Peleg] [from old catalog] [Aborn

A Descriptive and Historical Sketch of Boston Harbor and

Surroundings

Peleg] [from old catalog] [Aborn

A Descriptive and Historical Sketch of Boston Harbor and Surroundings

ISBN/EAN: 9783744760881

Printed in Europe, USA, Canada, Australia, Japan

Cover: Foto ©Andreas Hilbeck / pixelio.de

More available books at **www.hansebooks.com**

A

DESCRIPTIVE AND HISTORICAL

SKETCH

OF

BOSTON HARBOR

AND

SURROUNDINGS

GIVING

ALL THE ISLANDS, LEDGES, SHOALS, BUOYS,
CHANNELS, AND TOWNS FROM
NAHANT TO MINOT'S

WITH

Their Location and History

BOSTON
W. M. TENNEY AND COMPANY

INTRODUCTION.

As a rule, seaport towns have a fascination which
the most favored of inland municipalities cannot ap-
proximate ; for while the former are not hindered from
adorning themselves with all the graces of their inland
sisters, they have, besides, that atmosphere of direct
connection with remote quarters of the globe, which
appeals, not only to all imaginative natures, but also to
every one who is not a veritable Gradgrind at heart.
The editor of this sketch well remembers with what
joy he looked forward in his boyhood days to the
rare occasions when his father took him from a Con-
necticut town to visit New York for a day or two ; how
he wandered along the quays, weaving day-dreams ;
imagining that the grotesque figurehead of this vessel
had perhaps peered over the shores of a fragrant spice
island, or that mayhap a Polynesian cannibal had clam-
bered up the stern of another ; how he admired the
silent force of the liquid element that lazily swayed
these huge masses at their moorings ; and how, finally,
the vivid impressions of these scenes would last and

furnish him retrospective entertainment for weeks after his return to the paternal roof.

Attractive as seaport towns are, there are few more delightful than Boston, and its harbor is a very storehouse of natural beauties, historical reminiscences, and opportunities for healthful rational enjoyment. These advantages are becoming more appreciated from year to year, and to those who wish to enjoy its beauties the following pages are offered as a guide. While they can simply indicate the manifold points of interest which attach to each island, strait, and promontory, they will have achieved their mission if they but awaken the interest of the reader and point out his way for him.

𝔥istorical 𝔖ketch

OF

BOSTON HARBOR.

THE most southerly of the wharves which line the water front of Boston are used as landing-places for the numerous excursion steamers which ply the harbor. Embarking in one of these, let us ascend to the upper deck, and, before the start is made, take our bearings, and locate our surroundings. Looking eastward, we see the great area of flats lying between East Boston and Governor's Island. Nearest the chan- **Bird Island** nel are Bird Island Flats, named from the **Flats.** sunken island of which they form a part, and separated from Governor's Island by Governor's Island Channel. Beyond these, are Noddle's Island Flats, bearing the name originally given to the whole of East Boston. The harbor makes in somewhat here, forming a bay, dry at low water, bounded on the east by Winthrop, north by Breed's Island, and west by East Boston. South of Winthrop are Snake and Apple islands, bearing a few trees.

On our right are the docks on the newly filled flats of South Boston, which are separated from Boston proper by a channel running into the South Bay of Boston, known as Fort Point Channel.

The harbor here is narrow, with Boston and East Boston on either side, and extends to the **Navy Yard.** Navy Yard at Charlestown, which forms its extreme

limit.   The water within range of the eye from this
Inner point, inside and westward of Governor's
Harbor. and Castle Islands, is called the Inner
Harbor.

Starting on our excursion, the steamer takes the
Main Ship Channel, the deepest and best in the harbor, and the one used by all larger vessels.   The boundary lines are well marked by the United States government, and the channel has frequently been improved
by dredging.   The following brief description of the
buoys, and the laws governing the signals of vessels,
will be found useful as we proceed.

On entering a harbor the red buoys are always on
Buoys. the right or starboard side, and the black
buoys on the left or port side.   They are usually num-
bered from the mouth of the harbor.   Buoys are of
three kinds : spar, can, and nun buoys.   The nun buoys
are of three classes according to their size, and are
shaped thus. φ Can buoys are shaped thus. φ Buoys
painted red and black in horizontal stripes mark sunken
ledges or wrecks,   Steamers are required to give warn-
Steamer ing to others by whistle on which side they
Whistles. intend to pass : one blast to the starboard,
and two blasts to port.   Failure to comply with this
law makes the steamers liable to heavy damages, and
renders the pilot or sailing master liable to have his
license revoked.   Steamers must keep out of the way of
sailing vessels.   A steamer flying the United States
Mail Signal — a white burgee with the letters U. S.
M. — has more privileges than others.

On passing into the channel we leave on our right
Fort Point the flats forming the eastern boundary
Channel. the mouth of Fort Point Channel.   They
are quite extensive, extending from the city proper to
the extreme point of South Boston.   The first buoy on
Buoy No. 11, our course is the black spar buoy No. 11,
Slate Ledge. situated on the edge of the flats, and

marking Slate Ledge, which is dry at low water. From
this point to the city is a favorite anchorage ground for
many of the larger yachts. On the other side of the
channel is the site of the once famous Bird's Island,
now only a shoal, bare at low water, and marked on its
northeast end by an iron spindle with a red cage on top.
In early days this was a good-sized island, with a headland toward Governor's Island. In the narrow channel between, the tide swept with great swiftness. The
site of the headland is now marked by a red spar buoy,
No. 12, in twelve feet of water. In 1630 this island was
as large as Governor's Island, and in 1636 the General
Court granted a right for parties to mow the grass upon
its meadow. In April, 1658, we find a record that it
was "left to James Everill and Rich. Woody for sixty
years, paying 12d. silver, or a bushel of salt, in defect
of paym't att y' day 12d. or a bushel of salt for every
month's neglect." In 1726 a Frenchman who was
hanged in Charlestown was buried here and it was a
common burial-ground for criminals.

Governor's Island Channel has red buoy Red Buoy
No. 12 at the northern point of its en- No. 12.
trance, and black spar buoy No. 7 at the southern point.

GOVERNOR'S ISLAND.

Governor's Island is two
miles from Boston, and
half a mile from Castle Island. It was known in early
times as Conant's Island, being named from Richard

Conant, an early settler of Plymouth. It is of irregular shape, one mile long, and seventy feet high. In 1632 it was devised to Governor John Winthrop, and the rental was fixed at a hogshead of wine from the products of the island. It was greatly improved by the governor, and became a favorite resort, soon gaining the name of Governor's or Winthrop's Island. In 1696 two batteries were built, and in 1746 the island was still more thoroughly fortified. In 1808 it was sold to the General Government, and Fort Warren was erected on its summit, but later this name was given to the fort at the mouth of the harbor. In 1812 the fort was well garrisoned, and new defences were erected.

The present works were begun before the Civil War broke out, and were named Fort Winthrop. During that war the State militia did garrison duty here. The island contains seventy acres, with a moderate hill on its western side. This hill is crowned with a battery, and honeycombed by a network of subterranean passages. On the south side is a stone staircase to the water battery. The eastern side of the island is lowland. The Governor's Island Shoals make out on its eastern and northern sides. On the **Black Buoy No. 9.** opposite side of the channel is black nun buoy No. 9, situated on the northeast side of the shoal which makes off from South Boston. This vicinity is called the Upper Middle, and makes a bar that formerly almost extended across the channel. The highlands of South Boston (Dorchester Heights) are quite prominent from this point. On their summit is the large building of the Blind Asylum, while on the shore, almost in range, are the city buildings, House of Correction, and Lunatic Asylum. The extreme point of the peninsula is called City Point, off whose southern shore is moored the fleet of yachts belonging to the Boston and South Boston Clubs.

CASTLE ISLAND AND FORT INDE-
PENDENCE.

We now pass abreast of Castle Island, on which is Fort Independence. This island is situated two and one-half miles from Boston, and one mile from the main land, and its shores are protected by a sea wall. This island has for over two hundred and fifty years been the site of a fortification. In 1634 two platforms and a small earthwork were erected, under the superintendence of Roger Ludlow, of Dorchester, and its first commander was Capt. Nicholas Simpson, of the Ancient and Honorable Artillery Company. In 1638 the fort was abandoned by the government, and the island was leased to Captain Gibbons. The fortifications were kept up by the citizens of the surrounding towns till 1643. In 1650 the government again took it in charge, and renewed the old fortifications. A settlement of families was established, so as to form a resident garrison. At this time the fort frequently prevented disturbances between opposing foreign vessels. The castle was of brick, and had three rooms, — a dwelling below, a lodging room on the second floor, and a gun room over that. Boston erected a large bell upon its summit.

In 1661 Nicholas Upshall, under sentence for bring-
ing Quakers to Boston, was confined here. The fort
was struck by lightning in 1665, and its commander,
Capt. Davenport, was killed. In 1672 it was burnt,
and the following year the General Court rebuilt it from
funds raised by a tax levy of one shilling a ton on
every vessel of twelve tons burden entering the port
of Boston. This new fort was of stone; had four
bastions mounting thirty-eight guns, and under its
walls was a small stone battery of six guns. All passing vessels were required to lower their colors, and
those passing out had to show permits signed by the

Governor. In 1689 the Boston people seized the fort,
on account of the civil commotion in England, and
imprisoned within its walls King James's representative.
The old works were removed in 1701, and a new fort
of brick was built. The greater part of the cost of
these new works was borne by the English government, and the name, "Fort William and Mary," given
it. In 1691 the name was changed to Castle William,
in honor of King William III. Some parts of these
works remain to-day under the walls of the present
fortress.

From 1701 to the Revolutionary War (evacuation of

Boston) the fort was garrisoned principally by English troops. Its armament was strengthened at various times, and it is said that in 1750 the fort possessed one hundred guns. In 1764, barracks were erected for the accommodation of four hundred and eighty men, and here the American colonists received their first practical lessons in artillery practice, which, in after years, proved to them of much value. During the siege of Boston in 1776, the British considered this fort a coign of vantage, and turned its guns upon the Americans' fortification erected on Dorchester Heights, but a storm prevented the serious encounter, and wise councils led to the withdrawal of all the British troops in Boston Harbor. At this evacuation, March 17, 1776, the garrison destroyed the fort, and devastated the Island. In 1778 Congress rebuilt the works, and the garrison during the Revolution was mostly an invalid corps. Its barracks were used for recruits. From 1785 to 1805 the fort was used as a prison for State criminals. In 1798 Massachusetts ceded the island to the United States Government. The stronghold was named Fort Independence, in 1799, at the time of a visit of President John Adams. In 1803 a new fort was finished, with five bastions. During the war of 1812 it was garrisoned by Massachusetts militia. The present fortress was built in 1850. It has five sides, with guns in casemates, and large guns on top. It is built of granite. Inside of the enclosure is a large parade ground, while inside of the walls are the soldiers' quarters. Back of the fort, to the southwest, reached through a gateway, is a grassy plot, planted with trees, on which are erected a few houses used by the former officers. Near the west front of the fort is the old cemetery, where the remains of several of the old garrison are resting. The building on the south part of the island has been used as the Hospital. During the late Civil War this fort was garrisoned by many of the Boston militia companies. In 1863 the fort had one hundred and five cannon, and was the headquarters of the recruiting department of the State.

In 1881 the garrison was taken away and sent to Fort Warren, at the mouth of the harbor, for the reason stated by Gen. Hancock : " Concentration in one place is better for discipline." The fort, like its neighbor, Fort Winthrop, is only garrisoned at this time by a sergeant and a few men to keep things in repair. This fortress is the oldest post in the country, and it has been almost continuously occupied since its first erection, in 1634, to within a few years. It has never been besieged, and from its bastions have floated Gov. Endicott's flag, Cross of St. George (red cross on white field), Pine Tree (white Massachusetts flag), and the United States stars and stripes.

On the other side of the channel, about midway between Castle Island and Governor's Island, is a red **Red Buoy** nun buoy of the second class, No. 12. **No. 12.** It marks the northern point of the western entrance of the north channel of the Main Ship Channel. The southern point of entrance to this channel is marked by a red nun buoy of the third class, No. 10.
Lower Mid- The Lower Middle is an extensive shoal **dle Shoal.** lying E. S. E. by W. N. W., is one mile long, bare at mean low water. It lies in the middle of the channel. On its southern side, and about midway of its entire length, is the red first-class nun buoy No. 8, marking two small rocks which have six feet of water at low tide. These rocks are called State Ledge. Further beyond, and at the eastern extremity of the **Red Buoy** Lower Middle, is another red buoy, No. 6. **No. 6.** It marks the southern point of the eastern entrance of the Main Ship North Channel.

On the other — or south — side of the south Main Ship Channel is a black nun buoy of the second class, No. 7,

which is situated on the southeast point of the shoals
that make off from the southeast side of Castle Island,
extending to a distance of six hundred yards   These
shoals run around the island, south and west, to South
Boston Point.

PRESIDENT ROADS AND APPLE ISLAND.

We now enter into what is called President
Roads, formerly known as King's Roads.   It is also
sometimes designated as the Middle Harbor, — a wide
and good anchorage situated between Governor's
and Apple islands flats on the north, Deer Island on
the east, Long and Spectacle islands on the south,
and Castle and Governor's islands on the west.   It is
one and three fourths miles long, and nearly three
fourths of a mile wide.   On the north will be seen
Winthrop on the main land, whose southern point is
Point Shirley.   Northeast of Point Shirley is a small
island called Snake Island.   About three fourths of a
mile southwest from this island is another, called
Apple Island.   It contains about ten acres, is round
in shape, with the land gradually rising from the shore
to a height of fifty feet.   On its summit are seen a few
trees, said to be quite old.   The island takes its name
from its shape.   Extensive shoals surrounding this
island make it difficult of approach at low tide.   In the
earliest days of the colony this island belonged to Boston, and was used for pasturage.   It afterwards fell
into private hands, and, passing through various owner-
ships, during which it was highly cultivated, and a
handsome residence erected on it, it was purchased
in 1822 by William Marsh, who died here in 1833.
In conformity with his dying request he was buried
on the western side of the hill.   After being in neglect
for many years, the city of Boston bought the island in
1867 for $3,750.   It has never been occupied since,

but in recent years the water in its vicinity has been used as a site for burning old hulks, for the purpose of saving the iron and copper.

DEER ISLAND.

The large island forming the eastern boundary of President's Roads is Deer Island. It is four and one-half miles from Boston, and separated from Point Shirley by a narrow strait three hundred feet wide, called Shirley Gut, through which the waters of the inner harbor rush with immense velocity. The island contains one hundred and thirty-four acres of upland, and fifty acres of lowland; it is about one mile long, and about one third of a mile wide at its widest point, and has two hills and four bluffs. The highest of these hills is called Signal Hill. It has two fresh-water ponds. Extensive flats make out on the easterly side of the island. In 1840 the government built a sea wall to prevent the washing away of the land on the easterly side. The name Deer Island was given it, probably in Winthrop's time, from the great numbers of deer (deare) that fled to its shores to escape the attacks of the wolves. Densely wooded in these early times, it was a great game preserve for the colonists. April 1, 1634, Boston was granted this island, together with Long and Hog Island (Breed Island) for the small rent of two pounds, — afterwards reduced to two shillings, — with Spectacle Island thrown in; it has ever since remained under the same ownership. In 1675-6 Massachusetts used the island as a dwelling for the Christian Indians of the colonies during the Indian wars. A marauding party of the American army, in 1775, captured eight hundred sheep pastured here by the British.

A fortification was built upon the island in 1813 to protect Broad Sound. At this time it was a favorite picnic ground for the inhabitants of Boston. In 1850, city buildings were erected here at a cost of $150,000, and more were added in 1869. The large brick building crowned with a cupola is the House of Industry. The other buildings on the island are the House of Reformation, a school-house for truant boys, farm-house, bakery, workshops, a large piggery, and numerous smaller constructions. The island is highly cultivated both as a farm and garden. Deer Island is the northern limit of Boston Harbor entrance, **Broad Sound Channel Entrance.** while Point Allerton is the southern limit, The southern point of Deer Island is the entrance to Broad Sound: Nix's Mate and Long Island Head forming the southern point of entrance. A red pyramid, named Deer Island Point Beacon, marks a shoal which makes out a quarter of a mile from the extreme southern point of the island.

SPECTACLE ISLAND.

On the south of President Roads, looking to the southwest, we see Spectacle Island, and further beyond, Thompson's. The channel that runs to the westward of these islands is the entrance **Dorchester Bay Channel Entrance.** to Dorchester Bay (Neponset River). The channel to Quincy Bay has its entrance between Spectacle Island and Long Island Head **Quincy Bay Channel.** to the south, and the entrance to the

Western or Back Way channel is between Spectacle
Western, or Back Way. and Thompson's islands. Two high bluffs connected by a narrow isthmus form Spectacle Island and suggested its name. The northern hill is sixty-five feet high, with steep faces worn by action of the water. The southern hill is about the same height as the northern, and its faces are steep, except on its southern side, which is low and sandy. Both these islands are barren of trees, and are dotted with a few houses. This island is first mentioned in 1634, when it was granted to Boston with Deer, Long, and Hog islands at a rental of two shillings. In 1649 the town exacted a small rental from the settler of the island, but relinquished its right thereto in 1666, and soon after this, we find one Thomas Bill, a lighterman, purchasing the rights of the several owners. His son Samuel Bill, a butcher, was the first sole proprietor of the island ; at his death, in 1706, it was divided between his widow and son. In 1717 the government purchased a portion of the southerly end, and built a pest-house thereon. This station was removed to Rainsford Island in 1737. The whole of the island, in 1737, again came into possession of the Bill family, and it has remained in private hands ever since. For many years it was a pleasure-ground for excursion parties. A hotel was built here in 1847, and many families lived on the island during the warm season ; but the purchase of the island by Nahum Ward, in 1857, for the business of utilizing the carcases of horses, forever put an end to picnics and summerings on Spectacle Island.

THOMPSON'S ISLAND.

Thompson's Island is three miles from Boston, one mile from Fort Independence. It is one mile long and one third of a mile wide ; it rises in the centre to a hill seventy-five feet high, with a steep face to the north.

Its southern side terminates in a long, narrow, sandy
spit, extending to within one hundred feet of the main
land at Squantum. The group of buildings on the
height is the Farm School for Indigent Boys. The
west head has a grove of trees ; on the north and west
sides of the island the channels are deep, but, on the
south and east, flats make off for some distance. The
island was claimed in 1621 for David Thompson by
William Trevors, a sailor with John Smith ; it was first
named Island of Trevors, and afterwards Thompson's
Island. David Thompson was a Scottish gentleman,
who accompanied Capt. John Smith when the latter explored the harbor in 1619. Receiving a patent for considerable land about New England, from the Privy
Council in 1632, Thompson first settled at Piscataqua,
N. H., in 1623, with his family. In 1626 he settled upon
the island and established a trading-post for furs and
fish. It was the only island that had a harbor.
Thompson died in 1628, leaving the island to his wife
and infant son. In 1629 his widow returned to England. In 1634 Massachusetts granted the island to
Dorchester, but fourteen years later, young John
Thompson presented his prior claim, which was recognized by the government, and Thompson, after returning
to England, sold the island to two Bristol merchants.
For one hundred and fifty years after this, the island
was used for farming, the soil being the most fertile of
any in the harbor. In 1834 the Boston Farm School
Corporation purchased the island for $6,000, and it
was annexed to Boston. The present brick building, one hundred and sixty feet in length, was then
erected; the first floor contains the offices and dining
room, the second floor the school room, while the third
story is used as a dormitory. In 1882 a building containing a gymnasium and workshops was added. Here
the boys are taught the various trades, and help to run
the extensive farm connected with the school. The

history of the institution is darkened by a terrible calamity. In April, 1842, a large boat filled with the boys of the school, while on a pleasure trip down the harbor, was capsized by a sudden squall, and one hundred and twenty-three of the occupants were drowned.

LONG ISLAND.

Long Island is one and three fourths miles long and about one fourth mile wide, is situated about five miles from Boston, and one mile from Deer Island. It lies in a northeast and southwest direction, of undulating surface, and bare of trees except at the lighthouse and the hotel. On the northeast of the island is a hill about eighty feet high, with a bluff at its northern and eastern sides, which has been worn by the water, and is protected by a strong sea wall built by the government. From this hill the land gradually slopes down to a low pebbly beach ; then again rises to another hill ninety feet high, smooth and green, on whose northern side stands the large hotel, with numerous other buildings. From here, there is a series of hills varying in height, until the island terminates at its southwest end in a bare hill, fifty feet high, with steep sides. The island in early times was well wooded, and in 1634 was, as we have heretofore stated, deeded to Boston, with Deer, Spectacle, and Hog Islands for a rental of two shillings. Soon after, it was let to various persons, who made sad havoc with its forests. In 1639 the town divided it off to planters at a small rental, which was relinquished in 1667. In 1689 the title became vested in John Nelson, of Boston, and thereafter passed through various hands till 1849, when it was acquired by the Long Island Improvement Company, who built the hotel and wharf, and made several improvements, intending to make it an attractive summer resort. On the southern side of the beach, a cove makes in, forming a good harbor for small boats. During the present year — 1885 — the

LONG ISLAND LIGHT.

City of Boston has purchased the whole island, on which will be erected buildings for city purposes.

In 1775 the island was raided by the Continental soldiers, who drove off all the cattle and seventeen British sailors. They were pursued by the English boats, but made good their escape to Squantum.

LONG ISLAND LIGHT.

In 1819 a lighthouse was established on the northeast bluff by the United States government, and was refitted in 1851. The present lighthouse is an iron tower, thirty-five feet high, painted white, with a lantern painted black. It is of the fourth order of Fresnel, and visible seventeen miles. During the Civil War the island was a rendezvous for soldiers. The Ninth Massachusetts Regiment was encamped here, and sailed June, 1861, for Washington, D. C.

NIX'S MATE.

Passing outwards by Long Island Head, we see to our left the entrance of Broad Sound Channel, and to our right Nix's Mate, once an island, now reduced by the action of the sea to ,a sandy shoal, dry at low water. Its northern point is marked by a beacon, a black octagonal wooden pyramid resting on **Bell Buoy.** a granite base. On either side is a black spar buoy, No. 11, and the first-class black can buoy, No. 9, with an automatic bell buoy just inside of it. On the southern or further end of this shoal is a red spar buoy, No. 2, and a few yards off from it a black spar buoy, No. 3. These mark the channel which is used at high water by the Nantasket and Hingham steamers. We learn from an early record that this island in 1636 contained twelve acres of land, and was granted to John Gallop, and was used by his descendants as a pasturage for cattle up to the commencement of this century. The island was formerly used as a place for the execution of criminals. A somewhat apocryphal story is connected with the name of this island. About 1680 a pirate by the name of Capt. Nix landed here, buried his treasure, and murdered his companion to keep his secret secure. Another version of this story was that Capt. Nix's mate was hung here for murdering his captain ; that he protested his innocence, saying that if the island was ever washed away it would prove his innocence. There was an execution here in 1726, fully described in the *Boston News Letter* of July 14 of that year.

RAINSFORD ISLAND.

In looking down the channel, between Long Island and Nix's Mate, we see, some way down, Rainsford Island, by some called Hospital Island. It consists of two bluffs, connected by a narrow neck of land, and is the southern boundary of the entrance of the Western Channel, or Back Way. It is barren of trees, and on its northern bluff is erected a picturesque summer house. On the other side of the island are numerous buildings, used now as a home for paupers. Edward Rainsford, a prominent elder of the Old South Church, Boston, was its first settler (1636). He died on the island in 1683. After his death it passed through several hands, and in 1837 it was bought by the government, and used as a site for a hospital, or pest-house, till 1852, when it was used for quarantine purposes. From the early records we learn that in 1677 a vessel with smallpox on board anchored in the Nantasket Roads, which are off this island, and persons from the surrounding towns, boarding the vessel, spread the infection throughout the colony, over one thousand persons dying. From that time may be dated the first establishment of quarantine regulations. The highest bluff (that on the north) is known as Great Head (formerly Smallpox Point). In this bluff stands the old mansion house, built in 1819, which was famous for many years as a summer resort, the superintendent's house, the old Dead House, and other buildings. It also has a wharf. The West Head, or other bluff, has a long low building, called Fever Hospital, and the conspicuous building with columns is the Smallpox Hospital. On the southern part of the island is the old cemetery, containing old tombstones that mark the resting-places of many unfortunates. In former years Boston families sent their friends who were sick with contagious diseases to this island. In 1872 Boston bought the place, and converted it into an almshouse. After the Civil War the old veterans, or disabled soldiers, lived here until they were removed, in 1882, to their new home on Powderhorn Hill, Chelsea.

QUARANTINE GROUNDS.

This spot which we are now on, extending from the eastern side of Deer Island to the Ship Channel, is the water space known as the Quarantine Grounds. Here all vessels are required to come to anchor until they are visited by the port physician. The signal shown by the vessels is a flag flown on the shrouds. The doctor has a steamer (always known by the yellow flag). If there is sickness on board, dangerous to the public health, the vessels are obliged to remain a certain length of time to be sufficiently fumigated, and the sick unfortunates are carried to the hospital on the neighboring island.

LOVELL'S ISLAND.

After passing Nix's Mate we pass a red third-class nun buoy, No. 8, on what is called Seventy-four Bar, — a shoal that makes out from Lovell's Island. This island we pass on our left; it is three quarters of a mile long and one third of a mile wide, and is the flattest of any of the islands. A steep hill on the channel side is covered with grass, but the rest of the island is low, extending north, and making a point called Ram's Head. The island took its name, in 1630, from Captain William Lovell, of Dorchester, and it was noted in those early days for its immense amount of rabbits. Granted to Charlestown in 1648, and to Hull in 1654, it was sold in 1767 to Elisha Leavitt, of Hingham. In 1825 Boston bought this island, together with George's Island, for $6,000; at the present time it is used by the United States as a lighthouse supply station. The United States government built a sea-wall along its northern side (Ram's Head), in 1840. In 1782 the *Magnifique*, a French battle-ship, went ashore on this side and sank; it was reported that she had great treasures on board, and for many years people visited the site expecting to find the coveted loot. When the United States Engineers were dredging in 1859, they came across large quantities of lead, copper, and even cannon balls, twenty feet below the surface. Since that time the place has always been called Man-of-War Bar.

GALLOP'S ISLAND.

Upon the other side of the channel is Gallop's Island. It has a high, barren bluff on one side, and the other (eastern) side is low and sandy. In 1650 it was owned by Captain John Gallop, a pilot by profession, who had a farm here, a pasturage on Long Island, a sheep pasture on Nix's Mate, and a house in Boston. The soil was very fertile; and the island in early times was a noted supply place for ships. During the Revolutionary war, earthworks were erected on the bluff. In 1860 the city of Boston bought it for $6,600, and during the late civil war it was used as a rendezvous for soldiers, and numerous barracks were built. Since 1867 the island has been used as a quarantine hospital ground. Two hospitals, a dwelling for the doctor, and several other buildings were built. In 1868 a sea wall was built by the United States government on its south side. It has a pier, at which is frequently seen the quarantine steamer flying the yellow flag.

FORT WARREN.

We now come to George's Island, the site of Fort Warren. It is three hundred and fifty yards wide, and about six hundred yards long, and contains thirty-five acres ; now it is wholly occupied by the fort. It is situated between the main ship channel on the north, and Nantasket Roads and Western or Back Way on the south, and guards the entrance to Boston Harbor. In the colonial days it was used by the merchants' and war ships as a rendezvous. In 1778 the first fortification, consisting of a large earthwork, was erected by Count D'Estaing, the French Admiral, which, from its formidable array, prevented the British fleet, with Earl Howe and Sir Henry Clinton, from coming into the harbor. In 1833 the United States began the present fort, which was not finished till 1850.

General Thayer, for many years the Superintendent of West Point, was the designer. In 1840 the sea wall was built. In 1861, through the exertions of our cherished war governor, John A. Andrew, it was heavily armed and garrisoned by the Boston militia. During the civil war it was occupied by many of the well-known regiments and the famous war song, "John Brown," was composed and sung by members of the 24th regiment. Within the walls of this fort were imprisoned many noted men ; Mason and Slidell, and Alexander H. Stephens, Vice President of the Confederate States, among the number. In 1861-2 it had eight hundred Confederate prisoners. The walls of the fort are hammered granite with loop-holes for muskets. It has a moat fifty feet wide, and has outworks and water batteries. It is pentagonal in shape, with bastions at each angle, commanding the ditches, and encloses a space of five acres. The masonry is of great thickness, and the casemates contain the barracks, magazine, hospital, mess-rooms, etc. The faces of the fort are masked behind ramparts of earth, into which shot may sink without doing harm. Opposite George's Island on the other side of the channel is the entrance of Black Rock Channel, that **Black Rock Channel.** takes its name from a rock in the middle of the channel, and leads into Broad Sound.

BUG LIGHT.

Making out from Lovell's Island is a ledge of rocks called Whitney's Ledge. We now enter what is called the Narrows, so called from the narrowness of the channel here ; on our left is a curious lighthouse on seven stilts, called Bug Light, — a small house with a lantern in its centre, thirty-five feet from sea level. It shows a fixed red light visible twelve miles ; it also has a fog signal. This lighthouse was built in 1856, and is situated on a long sand bar that makes out one mile

from Great Brewster Island.   Near this light is a gran-
Spit Beacon. ite beacon called Spit Beacon, and further
beyond is another beacon, granite, with a spindle and
cage on top, painted red, called False Spit Beacon, and
marking the site of two rocks, since removed ; it also
marks the limit of the Narrows.   Opposite, and on the
right of the channel, we pass two other buoys. The first,
a black, thiid-class nun buoy, No. 7, marks a ledge of
rocks which makes off from George's Island.   The
other buoy, a second-class nun buoy, No. 5, marks a
ledge of rocks called Centurion Rocks, or the Centurion.   These rocks are marked in the Western or
Back Way Channel by a red nun buoy, No. 2, the
northern side of the entrance of Nantasket Roads.

NANTASKET ROADS.

We will now turn to our right, sail at a right angle
with our former course, and approach the entrance to
Hull or Hingham Bay. The channel which we will
pass through is that between George's Island Rocks
and the Centurion Rocks, and on the south of these
rocks, marking the Back Channel, is the second-class
red nun buoy No. 2.   This channel is sometimes used
by the Nantasket excursion steamers, but those most
frequently used are those between Long Island and
Nix's Mate Beacon, and the one on the other
side of George's Island (Fort Warren) and Gallop's
Island. After passing these rocks (George's Island
and Centurion) we sail directly across the Nantasket
Roads, and pass the outer entrance of Western or
Back Way, and approach Windmill Point, the western extremity of Hull. The buoy we see on our left,
just inside Hunt's Ledge, and nearer to the Hull shore,
is Toddy Rocks (a second-class black nun buoy, No. 1),
marking the entrance of Western Way. A prominent
Windmill   object on Windmill Point is Hotel Pem-
Point.   berton, built some four years ago by the

railroad company. The piazzas of this house command an animated water view, and have become a favorite resort for excursionists. This point of Hull is separated from Pettick's Island by Hull Gut, marked by a bell buoy at entrance, — a strait only about five hundred feet wide, through which the tide flows with great velocity, — so strong that it sometimes takes hours for a sailing vessel to make the passage.

PETTICK'S ISLAND.

Pettick's Island, sometimes called Paddock's Island, is two miles long, extending nearly to the Quincy shore, and forming the western boundary of Hull or Hingham Bay. The island is bare of trees. Its surface is undulating. Named, over two hundred and fifty years ago, after Lemuel Paddock, a French trader, it was granted to Charlestown for twenty years in 1624, but, before the lease expired, Hull became its possessor. In 1775 a number of continental troops were stationed here to defend the entrance of Boston Harbor. Three years later, in 1778, the French Admiral, Count d'Estaing. landed here, and erected some forts. The only tenant of the island is Mr. Samuel Cleverly, a pilot ; and with this exception, not a human soul is allowed to encamp upon its land. Several futile attempts have been made to procure building lots here.

HINGHAM BAY.

Inside this Hull Gut a most beautiful bay opens to view, over three miles long and two miles wide, dotted at its upper part by numerous small islands, and landlocked on all sides. Its waters offer an unusual attraction to yachtsmen. On the inside of Windmill Point are two long wharves, the first belonging to the Boston & Hingham Steamboat Co., and the other, at the foot of one of the hills of Hull, belongs to the Boston, Hingham, & Downer Landing Steamboat Co. On

HINGHAM BAY

this latter wharf is situated the handsome house of the Hull Yacht Club. This club, although the youngest in New England, having been incorporated in 1882, has shown the most activity of any organization, and now stands first in the United States, both as regards membership and number of yachts. Its regattas every week of the summer make the bay the scene of intense excitement.

The town of Hull is a popular summer resort for the inhabitants of Boston, and its many hills are thickly settled with many fine residences. Passing the hill of Hull, a cove makes in on the left to some distance. We notice here two spar buoys, **Buoys on** one black, No. 1, and one red, No. 2, mark- **Seal Rocks.** ing what is called the inner and outer Seal Rocks. This cove extends to Point Allerton, the head of Nantasket Beach. In range of this point we see a small island, called Hog Island. It is uninhabited, low, and surrounded by flats, dry at low water, and belongs to Hull. The whole shore on our left, as far as the eye can reach, is that famous beach, whose praises have been sung by all New England. Everything that the heart can long for is here, from the palatial hotel to the small shooting lodge, ocean bathing, and amusements of all kinds for young and old, while the invigorating breezes from old Neptune give new life to the hard toilers of the city and country.

BUMKIN ISLAND.

Proceeding on our course, we pass a black spar buoy, No. 1, marking a shoal that makes off from Bumkin Island just ahead of us. This little island is owned by Harvard College, which derives a small income from its pasturage. To our right is Sheep Island, nearly one mile from Bumkin Is- **Sheep** land. It is a low island of only two acres, **Island.**

and is fast being washed away. After passing these
islands we pass on our left a black spar buoy, No. 3,
marking a rock in the channel called Channel Rock,
and on our right a red spar buoy, No. 2, marking
shoals. These buoys are at the entrance, on our left,
Weir of Weir River, the passage for Nantasket
River. steamers. It is a picturesque but small
river, with well-wooded shores and winding channel.
After approaching near the beach, the river extends
back into the country ; a branch is used by the steamers for a landing on Nantasket beach. The entrance
to Weir River is between two hills : on the left White
Head, and on the right World's End, this latter joined
by another called Planter's Hill. These hills, together
with this shore, will be described later on, as well as
other points, on which we at present touch but lightly.
On our right, over half a mile distant, will be seen two
Slate islands. The smaller, and one nearest us,
Island. is Slate Island, so called from its slate quar-
ries, although not now much used. The whole shore
is lined with beds of this stone. It is a small island, of
about twelve acres, low, and has a few trees. A few
years ago a hermit lived on the island, but at present
it is uninhabited. Beyond this island is a much larger
one called Grape Island, which guards the entrance of
Weymouth Back River, and the eastern boundary of
Weymouth Fore River. It is half a mile long, and
has two hills on its northern side, and another on its
southern. Like all the islands in this bay it is surrounded by extensive flats. At the present time. or
till within a few years, its sole inhabitant was a weather-
beaten old fisherman, who very rarely allowed any
approach of a stranger. The high hill beyond this
island is Hough's Neck, or Quincy Great Hill, which,
with another small island at its foot, called Nut Island,
will be described further on when we reach Quincy
Bay.

We now enter the harbor of Hingham ; Planter's Hill on our left, and on our right Crow's Point, forming the boundaries of its entrance.

Off Crow's Point, on the edge of a shoal making off from the point, is a black spar buoy, No. 5. At this point several small islands will be noticed.

Black Spar No. 5.

HINGHAM BAY.

The first on the left is a low, rocky island called Chandler's Island. Hingham Harbor is about one mile long and about seven eighths of a mile wide. At low water it is nothing but a dry flat with a narrow, extremely crooked channel leading to the wharves in the town of Hingham. At Crow's Point the steamers make a landing. By the munificence of Samuel Downer, a Boston merchant, the once desolate shore is turned into a vast pleasure garden, called Downer Landing, visited by countless throngs during the summer months. Connected with this garden are Ragged and Sailor islands, small and rocky. They afford a pleasant resting-place for the weary pleasure-seeker. Farther within the harbor lie two other small islands in the middle of the flats. Button Island, the larger, is only about one hundred feet in diameter ; the smaller is called Beacon Island, from the beacon erected upon it.

Downer Landing.

Having made the exploration of Hingham Bay, we will retrace our steps to the Main Ship Channel, or, rather, to Nantasket Roads, where it joins the said channel. We have before spoken of the False Spit Beacon, Centurion Rocks, and Hunt's Ledge, and in passing out of the harbor the next mark we reach is red spar buoy, No. 6, which is situated on a ledge of rocks called Nash's Rock.

Red Spar No. 6.

THE BREWSTERS.

The land on our left is Great Brewster Island, the largest of seven islands or ledges at the mouth of Boston Harbor, all bearing the same name. It is said that all these once were one island. They derived their name, in 1621, from Elder Brewster, of the Plymouth Colony. Great Brewster, the innermost, contains twenty-five acres, and an immense spit or flat on the extremity of which is Narrows Lighthouse, or Bug Light, of which we have spoken elsewhere. It was bought by the City of Boston, in 1848, of Lemuel Brackett. The island is a high bluff, half washed or eaten away by the sea, has a sea wall built by the government, and a stone wharf. On its summit stands a handsome dwelling, erected and owned by Benjamin Deane of Boston. The island is grassy, and, by the care of its tenant, presents many pleasing aspects.

BOSTON LIGHT.

Little Brewster, sometimes called Lighthouse Island, and, in early days, Beacon Island, was taken for its present purpose. As early as 1679 a beacon was erected. In 1713 the government built the first lighthouse, and, in fact, it claims the honor of being the first lighthouse ever built in the United States. In 1757 it was rebuilt at a cost of £2,385, 17s. 8½d., and was maintained by a tax of one penny a ton on all vessels passing in or out. At the commencement of the Revolutionary War, the island was slightly fortified. We learn that in 1775 some Continental troops landed on Great Brewster and destroyed the lighthouse, and on another day of the same year a more serious attack was made; the fort was stormed, many of the garrison were wounded, and cannon and soldiers were captured. The present lighthouse was

BOSTON LIGHT.

built in 1783, and is eighty-six feet high and one hundred
and eleven feet above sea level. It is a white revolving
light, visible sixteen miles, and is classed as second of
order, Fresnel. Connected with the light is a steam fog-
horn, which in foggy weather gives blasts of seven seconds' duration at intervals of fifty-three seconds. The
first keeper of this lighthouse was George Worthlake,
who was drowned off Noddle Island, and is the subject
of the famous "Lighthouse Tragedy," a poem written
Middle   by Benjamin Franklin. Middle Brewster
Brewster. is a high, rocky island of ten acres. Behind one of the cliffs is the summer residence of one of
the well-known Boston lawyers, Augustus Russ. The
passage between this island and the outer island is very
dangerous, and is called the Flying Place. In a storm
the roar of the sea is tremendous. Six hundred feet
from this island is the Outer Brewster, a very rocky
island, possessing a few acres of good soil. It has a
spring of fresh water and a pond. In 1840 the island
was inhabited by three or four persons, and they had
six head of cattle and fifty sheep. In 1861 a fisherman
and his family lived there, and some little time later he
was drowned, and his family left the island. The approach to this island is fraught with danger, and no
cove offers any shelter from the angry waves. Beyond
the Outer Brewster are Tewksbury Rocks, and still
further Martin's Ledge ; the former not buoyed, and
the latter has a red second-class nun buoy, No. 2.
They have deep water around them, and are only dangerous to large vessels.

SHAG ROCKS.

The ledge of rocks outside of Boston Light, or Little Brewster, and south of Middle Brewster, are called
Shag Rocks, a group of rocks, twenty or twenty-five
feet above water, pretty bold, and extending some distance. This is the scene of many shipwrecks. In

1861 a ship was driven ashore, and soon after went
to pieces; thirteen of the crew were rescued by
Hull fishermen after clinging to the bare rocks for
over twenty-four hours; twenty-five others perished
before succor arrived.   Further beyond this ledge,
and one third of a mile from Outer Brewster to the
sea, is another ledge called Boston Ledge, a mass
of rocks eleven feet below the surface of the water,
marked by a red second-class nun buoy, No. 4. These
islands and rocks separate the Main Ship Channel
from Broad Sound Channel, and form the northern
boundary of the entrance to the main channel, which is
one and one eighth mile wide here ; directly opposite, on
the other side of the channel, is a beacon, and second-
class black nun buoy, No. 3, on a shoal **Black Nun
No. 3.**
that makes out two hundred feet from the
shore.   The first, is a pyramidical granite beacon, surmounted by an iron shaft with a black cone on top.

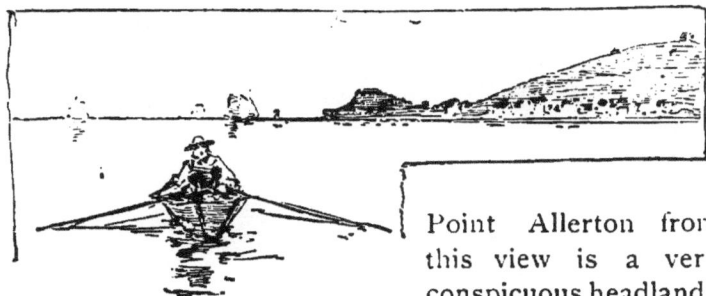

Point   Allerton   from
this view is a very
conspicuous headland ;
it is a bare hill one hundred and fifteen feet high,
with steep sides which have been much washed by
the sea.   Its sides are now protected by a massive
sea wall erected by the United States government.

We now shape our course south, following the shore
of Nantasket Beach.   Two and a quarter miles seaward from Point Allerton, on our left, on this new
course, is a ledge of rocks twenty-seven feet (four and
one half fathoms) below the surface of the water,

which are called The Thieves, or Thieves' Ledge. Continuing on our present course, we pass a bell boat known as Harding's Bell Buoy (iron, with bell weighing five hundred pounds, twelve feet from level of sea, with the name of the ledge in white letters below it). The action of the waves swaying the boat tolls the

HARDING'S LEDGE.

bell. It is placed three hundred feet from the north point of an extensive ledge of rocks known as Harding's Ledge, and formerly known as Conyhasset Rock. This ledge is three eighths of a mile square, and is half a mile from the main land, and a mile and an eighth from Thieves' Ledge. On its inside edge is an iron beacon thirty one and a half feet high, surmounted by an iron ring or wheel, four feet in diameter, set horizontally with twelve wooden pendants, five feet long, attached to the rim, the whole being painted black. Between this ledge and the shore there is a passage, but only used for small vessels. The first hill we see rising from the beach on our right is Strawberry Hill, a smooth green hill one hundred feet high, bare of trees. Next is a smaller hill forty-five feet high, called White Head, and further along is another called Sagamore Hill, eighty feet high and also treeless. The coast from here makes out towards the sea. At the point where it leaves the beach is a prominent hill covered with fine summer residences and a large hotel called the Atlantic House. This hill is called Atlantic Hill, eighty to ninety feet high ; its shore is bold and rocky. Next comes Green Hill ; its aspect is similar to the last named, and is about fifty feet high. The two barren rocks that are now seen a little way from the shore are known as Black Rocks ; on the larger of the two is a private shooting lodge. The fishing at this point is excellent, and in autumn there is sometimes good duck-shooting. The shore of the main land extends out to within a mile and a half of Minot's Light, then turns abruptly south to the harbor of Cohasset. The town of Cohasset comprises all the land east and south of Green Hill. On the northern shore of this point there formerly was a large cove, which was then used as the old harbor of Cohasset, but of late years a sandy beach has been formed across its entrance, and the new harbor is all that is used at present.

MINOT'S LIGHT.

We now approach a whole nest of rocks and sunken ledges ; on the outermost one, called Minot's Ledge, is built a noted lighthouse called Minot's Light, — a tall gray tower, built of granite, with bronze lantern,

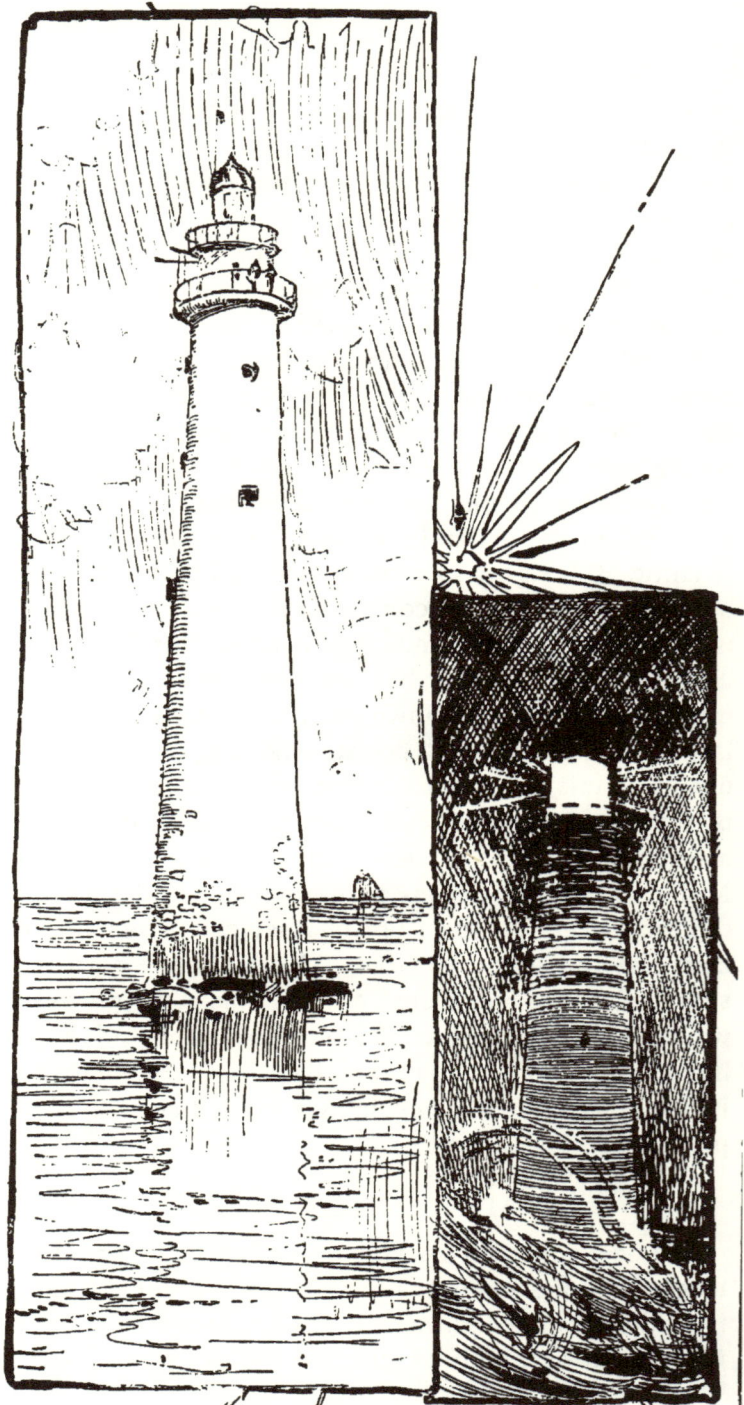

MINOT'S LIGHT.

one hundred feet above the sea, of the second order of Fresnel, with a fixed white light visible sixteen miles. For foggy weather a bell is struck by machinery. This present lighthouse was commenced July 1, 1855, and was not finished until 1859. The work was one of much difficulty owing to the constant action of the sea. The old lighthouse was built on stilts, and was washed away during the disastrous storm of April 15, 1851. The light is now kept by a relay of four men, two in a watch of two weeks. They are not allowed to go ashore, and delight in the occasional visits of excursionists.

The collective name of the nest of rocks, of which Minot's Ledge is the outermost, is Cohasset Rocks. Between some of these ledges is a passage for vessels, called Gangway Passage, but as it is fraught with danger it is seldom used. Eastward of Minot's Ledge is a second-class black nun buoy, No. 1, marking a rock called Davis' Ledge ; there is no passage between it and Minot's. The shore from this point south has but little interest, so we will return to Boston Light, the entrance to Boston Harbor, proceed north, and return to the city through Broad Sound. After passing the outer Brewster Island, Tewksbury Rock, and Martin's Ledge, we see to our left a low grassy island dotted with a few trees, called Calf Island. Calf Island. It seems to join the Middle Brewster, but is really five hundred feet distant from the Brewster, with a shoal passage. Formerly an excursion point, it is now seldom visited except by fishermen. A small distance to the eastward is a rock called Pope's Rock. Almost one hundred feet from this island, connected with a shoal, is another small rocky island called Little Calf Island. Still further beyond is Green Island, three eighths of a mile north of Little Calf Island ; it is of moderate height, with a white rock on its eastern side, with a small area of grass, and a long gravelly point south, from which extends a line of small rocks for three hundred and fifty yards.

Between Green Island and Little Calf Island lies Hypocrite Channel. It has many sunken ledges, not buoyed, and is seldom used except by small vessels. It is the most direct outlet for the Black Rock Channel between Lovell's Island and Narrows lighthouse, and sometimes is used to lessen the distance in entering Broad Sound Channel. The ledges in Hypocrite Channel will be described after we enter Broad Sound. About seven hundred yards to the eastward (seaward) from Green Island are a number of small **Roaring** rocks, some bare at low water, called the **Bulls.** Roaring Bulls, sometimes called Sunken Rocks, they taking their name from the roar the waves make in rushing and breaking over their surface. A passage exists between them and Green Island. A considerable way out to sea, from this point, lies a very dangerous ledge of bare rocks, six hundred yards in **The Graves.** length, called the Graves, after Thomas Graves, Vice-Admiral of Winthrop's fleet, a noted engineer and sailing-master, who planned the first settlement of Charlestown. Four hundred and fifty yards northeast from these rocks is Northeast Grave, a small but dangerous rock, exposed only at low water. It is **Whistling** marked by a whistling buoy, an automatic **Buoy.** whistle placed upon a nun buoy, which, by the action of the waves, produces a most dismal sound. The buoy is placed some four hundred yards from the rock.

BROAD SOUND.

We will now enter Broad Sound, passing the Graves on our right hand and the Roaring Bulls to the left. The rocky peninsula of Nahant looms up in the north, with the adjacent city and harbor of Lynn. The further shore comprises Revere Beach and Winthrop,

with Deer Island near by.   When abreast of Green
Island, about one fourth of a mile this side (north), is
a detached rock, eighteen feet below the surface, called
Maffit's Ledge : it is not buoyed.   A quarter of a mile
past this ledge is another detached rock, fifteen feet
below the surface, not buoyed, and called Commissioners' Ledge.   Between these two ledges, some little
distance off, and beyond Green Island can be seen a
red spar buoy, No. 2.   This marks a ledge   Red Spar
of rocks directly in the middle of Hypocrite   No. 2.
Channel, which enters between Calf and Green islands.
These rocks are called Half Tide Rocks. and are particularly dangerous, having only two feet of water over
them.   Beyond Commissioners' Ledge we pass Devil's
Back, a ledge of rocks nearly five hundred feet long and
extremely dangerous, some being bare at low water.
They are marked by a black first-class nun   Black Nun
buoy, No. 1.   Still further beyond this ledge   No. 1.
is another, called Alderidge's Ledge, and is marked by
a black second-class nun buoy, No. 3.   This ledge
separates Hypocrite from Broad Sound Channel.   Between this ledge and Half Tide Rocks is a series of
shoals, one of which is called Twelve-Foot Rock, so
named on account of the depth of water.   From this
point we look towards the left, and see, beyond, the
back side (northern) of Brewster islands, and the long
spit running off from the Great Brewster, with Bug
Light at its end.   We now approach the extensive
shoal making off from Lovell's Island, on which the
French frigate Magnifique, was wrecked.   On its
outer end, called Ram's Head, is placed a black second-
class nun buoy, No. 5.   On the opposite side of Broad
Sound Channel is Deer Island.   On the shoals extending out from the island are placed two red buoys and
a beacon.   The innermost one is on the shoal called
Little Fawn Bar, a red second-class   Red Nuns,
nun buoy, No. 4.   The outermost bar is   Nos. 4 & 2.

called Great Fawn Bar.   On the outer edge is placed
a red second-class nun buoy, No. 2.   Two thirds
of a mile inside this buoy is placed a red conical beacon of stone, with an iron spindle and cage on top.   A
channel passes over this shoal between the beacon
and buoy, which is called the North Channel of Broad
Sound, while the channel which we have used is called
the South Channel.

We are now on the Quarantine Grounds, hitherto
described.   Broad Sound here joins the Main Ship
Channel between Deer Island and Long Island.
Having described this channel elsewhere, we will
pass through the North Channel of Broad Sound,
over the shoals of Great Fawn Bar, and approach Winthrop Great Head.   Here a shoal makes out from the
main land, and its outer edge is marked by a red spar
buoy, No. 2.   It is also the northern boundary of the
entrance to Shirley Gut Channel, a channel but seldom
used, on account of the swift currents, and then only by
steamers of light draught.   Entering this channel, and
sailing towards the city of Boston, we approach the
Black Spar Shirley Shore, and see ahead of us a black
No. 1.   spar buoy, No. 1, on a shoal that makes
out from Deer Island.   The channel here is very
narrow and crooked, only about fifty feet wide, and
makes a sharp turn at right angles.   The current
is very strong ;   only a steamer or a yacht with a
strong wind can stem it.   The land on either side is
pebbly and on the Shirley shore, close to the water, is
the ever famous hostelry kept by O. A. Taft, whose
bird and fish dinners have a national reputation.   After
passing out of this Shirley Gut, a broad expanse of
shoals meets our view, the same that we saw when first
embarking on our steamer.   Those on our left are
Deer Island shoals.   Those on our right are Apple
Island shoals, with the island of the same name in the
centre ; and further beyond, to our right, are the exten-

sive shoals making off from East Boston, called Noddle's Island shoals. On this end of Apple Island shoals, between them and Deer Island shoals, is placed a red spar buoy, No. 6. Here, at this point, this channel joins that of Governor's Island Channel, where it has its entrance from the Main Ship Channel.

GOVERNOR'S ISLAND CHANNEL.

Governor's Island Channel is not much used, particularly at this entrance, but at its other entrance it is occasionally made use of by the excursion steamer that plies between Winthrop and Boston. The entrance of the channel with Main Ship Channel is marked by two red spar buoys, Nos. 2 and 4, situated upon a shoal in the middle of the channel's entrance, called the Middle Ground (different from the Lower Middle of the Ship Channel). This divides the channel into two entrances, the western one being the only one buoyed. On the other side of this western entrance are the extensive shoals making out from Governor's Island. Their extreme point is marked by a black spar buoy, No. 1. Leaving the entrance of Shirley Gut Channel, we follow Governor's Island Channel between the shoals — Apple Island on our right, and Governor's Island on our left — until we reach, on **Red Spar** our right, red spar buoy No. 8, on the **No. 8.** western spit of the first-named shoal. On our left, some little distance beyond, is a black spar buoy, No. 3, marking the northern point of Governor's Island shoal. Here the channel begins to bend, and ahead of us, on Noddle's Island shoal, is a red spar buoy No. 10. The flats on our left, extending from Governor's Island, are called Glade Flats ; on the northern part **Glade** of these is a black spar buoy, No 5. Our **Flats.** course from here is directly to the Main Ship Channel in the inner harbor, which is marked by the red

beacon or spindle, and red spar buoy No. 12 on
Black Spar our right, on Bird Island shoal, and on
No. 7. our left by black spar buoy, No 7, on
Governor's Island western shoal.

DORCHESTER BAY.

We have now reached our starting point, after having made a survey of all the islands and shoals of the
Main Ship Channel and the minor channels adjoining.
Three other passages alone remain to be visited, viz.
Dorchester Bay, Quincy Bay, and Lynn Harbor. We
will first visit Dorchester Bay. Passing once more be-
tween Governor's and Castle islands, we turn to our
right, and proceed through the Ship Channel towards
Neponset River. The entrance to this bay lies between
Castle and Spectacle islands. The bay itself is quite
large, and contains extensive flats, through which the
narrow channel runs close to the shore of Thompson's
Island and Squantum, to the mouth of Neponset River.
The main land boundary is the whole of Dorchester,
extending from South Boston, formerly Dorchester
Heights, where it almost reaches Fort Independence,
to the extreme southern portion known as Squantum,
— the special districts being Cow Pasture, Savin Hill,
Harrison Square or Commercial Point, and Neponset,
with the high land of Mount Bowdoin and Meeting-
House Hill forming the background. This bay, on
any summer afternoon, is a resort for many of the trim
little yachts belonging to Boston and Dorchester.
The first mark which we reach after entering the
Old Harbor channel is red spar buoy No. 2, situated
Shoals. on the outer edge of an extensive shoal
called Old Harbor Shoals, which makes out from South
Boston and Cow Pasture Point. All these shoals
comprise what was once the Old Harbor of the first
settlement of Dorchester. Off from the further end

of Thompson's Island (which we pass to our left), upon
a short shoal, is black spar buoy No. 1, and on the
opposite side of the channel is a red spar buoy, No.
4, and, further along, another red spar buoy, No. 6,
marking a portion of the shoals of Old Harbor and
Cow Pasture. On our left we see abreast of us the
high bluff of the Squantum peninsula, now belonging to the town of Quincy. From the channel to this
basin is one vast shoal. Under the bottom of the bay
lies the tunnel of the new sewerage sys- **Sewer**
tem of the city of Boston, which extends **Tunnel.**
from Cow Pasture Point, where the Pumping Station
is situated, to Moon Island. just the other side of
Squantum. Our course is now close to Savin Hill.
Here we note a black spar buoy, No. 3, on our left,
marking Farm Point Shoals. Here the channel makes
an abrupt turn to Commercial Point. On the left of
the channel at this point is a rock bare at low water,
called Half Tide Rock. The mouth of Neponset River
is bounded on the north by Commercial Point, and on
the south by Farm Meadows. The river is navigable
to the village of Neponset, one mile from its mouth,
and is supplied with five spar buoys, marking Tilston's
Flats, Chatman's Flats, Minot's Point Flats, Wood's
Point Flats, and Seal Rock.

We will now retrace our course to the head of
Thompson's Island and enter the channel called Western or Back Way, its entrance being between this
island on our right and Spectacle Island on our left.
This channel is often used by vessels to escape the
strong current of the Main Ship Channel. On our
right, extensive shoals make out nearly three quarters
of a mile from Thompson's Island. Abreast of their
easternmost point, and on the right of the channel, a
ledge of rocks, called Sculpin Ledge, is marked by a
red spar buoy, No. 2. These are in the channel of the
same name, which follows the shore of Long Island

until it enters Main Ship Channel. Our course is now between Long Island on our left, and Moon Island on our right. This island is three quarters of a mile long, with a high hill or bluff on this side of it, bare of trees. The rest of the island is low, terminating in a spit or bar reaching to the peninsula of Squantum. The buildings or masonry we see are the outlet and reservoir of the Boston sewerage system. On the further side of Moon Island, close to the peninsula, is a very small, low island, hardly ever recognized. We have now entered the waters of Quincy Bay, but, before mentioning this bay, we will continue following the Western or Back Way. This Western passage now turns abruptly to the north, between Long Island on the left and Rainsford Island on the right, then turns again, leaving Nix's Mate passage and George's Island on the left. Nantasket Roads are now entered, and the course is a straight one, being the same as taken before, after leaving Hingham Bay for the trip to Minot's Light.

QUINCY BAY.

Quincy Bay is very large and somewhat shallow, two and a half miles wide and one mile long. It is bounded on the east by Pettick's Island and Hough's Neck, south by the shore of Quincy, and on the west by Squantum and Thompson's Island. South of Rainsford Island, and in this bay, is the extensive ledge, partly bare at low water, called Quarantine Rocks, which makes out five eighths of a mile south from the shore of this island, and, not being buoyed, forms a dangerous obstacle, particularly to small boats or yachts. Further beyond, and to the south, is a ledge of rocks,

Sunken Island Beacon. dry at low water, called Sunken Island, or Sunken Ledge. It is marked by an open-work beacon with granite base, surmounted with a wooden staff and cage painted black.

A little to the westward and south of this island is another dangerous ledge of rocks, called Hangman's Island ; so named, it is said, from an execution that took place upon the island before it was washed away. The island is now only seven feet out of water and surrounded by dangerous shoals. After passing Sunken Island we pass a red spar buoy, No. 4, on our right, marking Wreck Rock, a dangerous sunken ledge, three feet below the surface. It takes its name from being the site of a wreck, the timbers of which remained visible for many years. We are now abreast of the high bluff called Prince's Head, connected **Prince's** with the lower end of Pettick's Island by **Head.** a spit or sand bar covered at high water. Opposite this head is Pig Rock Beacon, a wooden staff and cage painted black, on a granite base. It marks a dangerous rock lying on the edge of a flat in Hingham Bay, called Quincy Great Hill Flats. Quincy Great Hill is the high bluff at the end of the peninsula, called Hough's Neck, which forms the boundary of Quincy Bay, and belongs to the town of Quincy. Off the Hingham side of this peninsula, and connected with it at low water, is a small island called Raccoon Island. Op- **Raccoon** posite this island is a ledge of rocks called **Island.** Jack-knife Ledge, both being at the mouth of Weymouth Fore River. Situated on the flats at the foot of Quincy Great Hill, and connected with the bluff at low water, is Little Nut Island. **Nut Island.** It is treeless, with a hill sixty feet high, and was, up to within three years, the station of the United States government for the testing of heavy ordinance, which was aimed at a heavy target placed upon the bluff of Prince's Head. Upon the flats, close to the Quincy shore, is Half Moon Island, a crescent-shaped, sandy shoal or bank, ten feet out at low water, and covered at high water.

LYNN HARBOR.

Having now finished all the harbor of Boston, we will visit the harbor of Lynn, situated on the extreme northeastern point of Boston Bay. It is also on the north side of Broad Sound. The entrance is between West or Bass Point of the Nahant peninsula, and Chelsea or Revere Beach. It is full of rocks and shoals. Its channel is narrow, extending for the most part close to the shore of Lynn Beach or Nahant Peninsula. This peninsula is a long tongue of land extending some distance into the bay; its shores are very bold and rocky. Off Nahant Head, its outermost point, are several ledges of rocks, not buoyed, one of which is called Great Ledge. The western edge of the head is marked by a rocky islet, one hundred and fifty yards distant, called Pea Island, no passage between. Outside of this island is a group of dry rocks called Shag Rocks. These are not buoyed. A passage can be made between them and the island. On passing the western side of Nahant Head, we pass a sunken rock, three feet below water, called Joe Beach's Ledge, three hundred and fifty yards from Pea Island. It is marked by black spar buoy No. 1. To the left of this ledge is another, called Bass Rock, or Old Sunken Rock. It is bare at half tide, and marked by a red iron spindle with cage on top. Between this rock and the shore is a ledge of rocks called Bayley's Ledge, not buoyed. Beyond is Bass Point, the boundary of entrance to Lynn Harbor. Off the shore, some way up the harbor, beyond the point and off the west cliff, is a rock, dry at low water, called Old Harry's Rock. Abreast of it is a ledge called Lobster Rocks, bare at low water and surrounded by extensive shoals. This ledge is marked by a red spar buoy No. 2, and separates the channel into two, the east and west channels. The western channel is the most used. In proceeding up this channel we pass a red and black spar buoy with two prongs. It marks a number of rocks almost visible at low water, called White Rocks. Further up the channel we pass another red spar buoy, No. 4, marking a series of rocks, sometimes bare at extreme tides, called Black Rocks. These rocks are situated at the junction of the east and west channels. We now pass a dry flat upon our right, which separates the Lynn Channel from the Saugus River Channel. The shoal which makes out from this flat is called Forked Point Shoal, and sometimes Sandy Point. It is marked by a black spar buoy, No. 3. The last buoy in the channel is black spar buoy No. 5, marking Black Marsh. The shores of Lynn Harbor are low and marshy. Extensive flats make out in all directions, thereby making the entrance particularly difficult.

Having seen and described all the islands in and around Boston Harbor, we now will give a general description of the harbor itself.

BOSTON BAY.

The earliest accounts of explorations of this region that we have are semi-mythical traditions of Norse discovery.

This name has been given to the indentation lying between the headlands of Nahant on the north, and Point Allerton on the south. It is eleven miles wide, and extends inland for nearly seven and a half miles, and comprises the harbors of Boston, Dorchester, Quincy, Hingham, and Lynn.

BOSTON HARBOR

comprises all the water lying inside or west of the headlands of Deer Island on the north, and Point

Allerton on the south ; it is three and three quarters miles wide at its widest part, and its surface is dotted with numerous islands, through or around which there are many channels, which have been heretofore mentioned. This harbor is sometimes subdivided into Upper, Middle and Lower harbors, — Upper Harbor lying inside of Governor's and Castle Islands ; Middle Harbor between those islands and the Narrows ; and the Lower, or Outer Harbor, all beyond the Narrows.

The first explorers of the harbor are supposed to have been French fishermen from Acadia, who frequently visited it in the early part of the seventeenth century, for the valuable fishing and for the lucrative trade in furs with the Indians. As early as 1617 a French trading vessel was attacked and burned by the Indians, while at anchor off Pettick's Island, and, years after, French coin was dug up at Dorchester, bearing these early dates.

The first explorer of the harbor known to history was Captain John Smith, in 1614, but he, it is said, did not come inside of Point Allerton. The title rests with Miles Standish, of the Plymouth Colony. Sept. 29, 1624, he, with a small party, sailed from Plymouth in an open boat, on a mission to establish friendly relations with the Massachusetts Indians. They entered the harbor and anchored, the first night, off what is now known as Thompson's Island (some historians give Point Allerton as their place of anchorage), the next day they visited the main land in search of the Indian chief. landing at the mouth of what is now Neponset River. They were told that the chief was at Mystic (Medford) ; they crossed the harbor, and landed at what is now Charlestown, where they anchored. On the next day they went in search of the chief, travelling in the interior as far as Medford. They were unsuccessful and returned to their boat and sailed the next day for home.

The settlements around the harbor in the few next years were many. In 1630 Boston was settled by Governor John Winthrop, and from this time the events clustered around its waters are full of interest, and will be touched upon further on.

Boston Harbor, for commerce, is one of the best in the world, land-locked, interspersed with numerous islands, commodious, and with deep channels sufficient for the largest vessel. In time of war its defences would be almost impregnable, guarded at its mouth by high lands and a well and strongly built fortress. For beauty it cannot be excelled. Its many verdure-clad islands, its waters dotted by all kinds of sailing-craft. from the smallest yacht to the majestic ocean steamer, the whole surrounded by noble hills, unite to make a scene of surpassing interest and loveliness.

RAMBLES ALONG THE SHORES.

Starting from the northeastern point of Boston Bay, or, rather, from the main land just north of this point, we find the long peninsula of Nahant. This peninsula is composed of two unequal parts, called Nahant and Little Nahant, joined by a narrow strip of beach. The whole peninsula joins the main land by a sandy beach, called Lynn Beach, one and a quarter miles long. Little Nahant, the inner part of the peninsula, is a rocky bluff, eighty feet high. The beach connecting this bluff with the outer peninsula is half a mile long, and barely wide enough for the road extending along its surface. Nahant proper lies in an east and west direction, is high and rocky, with a high bluff on its eastern side, known as Eastern Point. Nahant has always been a favorite sea-shore residence for many of the wealthy families of Boston. Its fine location and grand sea view cannot be surpassed. Seven

eighths of a mile eastward of Eastern Point is a small,
rocky island called Egg Rock, sixty feet high, surrounded by deep water, and surmounted by a lighthouse.
Leaving Eastern Point, the shore runs in to the northwest, forming a cove called Nahant Harbor, its other
boundary being a hill called Bailey's Hill. From here
the shore runs in a westwardly direction to a point called
Bass Point, low lands, with high ground back of it.
The land between these two points is occupied as a
camping ground for parties from the interior towns.
From Bass Point we come to a bluff called the West
Cliffs ; its shore is steep and rocky. Thence the shore
runs north, by Little Nahant and Lynn Beach, on to
the main land, where is situated the city of Lynn. At
the point where Nahant joins the main land, the Lynn
Yacht Club has its club house, and at anchor in the
bay lie the yachts of its fleet. This organization is one
of the oldest in New England. At the present time it
has a membership of seventy-five, and a fleet of twenty-
five yachts. Nahant, originally called Pye Bay, and
by the Indians Mean's Island, belonged to the Indians
many years after Salem and Lynn were settled. It
was purchased in 1630 from the Indians, by a farmer
called Thomas Dexter, for a suit of clothes, but there
being some question about the purchase, it was again
sold for two pestle-stones. Well wooded in early times,
the peninsula was divided up in 1656, and each owner
was required, under penalty, to clear his share. It
then served for many years as a pasturage to the near-
lying towns. Joining Nahant, with a narrow neck of
beach, one and a half miles long, is the city of Lynn,
ten miles from Boston. It formerly comprised a vast
territory, composed of small settlements, which grew to
be towns and took upon themselves their own government. At the close of the Revolutionary War, Lynn
town possessed two thousand inhabitants, comprised
within the districts of Lynn, Lynnfield, Saugus,

Swampscott, and Nahant. Lynn was first settled in June, 1629, by parties from the settlement at Salem; it was called Saugust. By act of the General Court of 1637, given at the time Boston and other towns were named, the name was changed by this simple wording: "Saugust is Lin." It is supposed that the name was derived from Lynn Regis, in England, the birth-place of Samuel Whiting, one of its early ministers of the gospel. This settlement boasts as having among its early settlers the ancestors of the late Theodore Parker the theologian, and George Bancroft the historian. It also had among its number Daniel Howe, the first lieutenant of the Ancient and Honorable Artillery Company, of Boston, that was organized in 1638.

In 1643, iron works were erected upon the banks of the Saugus River, claimed by some to be the first ever built in America. It was here that the first coins of America were minted, and the first scythe and the first fire-engine made. In 1646 Lynn was the market town of the district. Here the farmers brought their produce and exchanged it for the products of the sea.

In 1750 John Adam Dagyr, a Welsh shoemaker, settled here, and through his energy he became known as the celebrated shoemaker of Essex, and gave the town the prestige that it still holds to-day. According to the *Boston Gazette* of 1764, the shoes manufactured here exceeded those imported, in strength and beauty. This industry received another impetus, after the Revolution, in the person of Ebenezer Breed, who introduced the use of morocco. It seems strange that both these men, who might be called the fathers of the shoe industry in America, died in poverty at the almshouse. Lynnfield was set off in 1814, Saugus followed in 1815, Swampscott in 1852, and Nahant in 1853. Lynn was made a city May 14, 1850. Many parts of Lynn have high ground, possessing fine and picturesque scenery, — Pirate's Glen, Dungeon Rock, and High Rock, the latter one hundred and seventy feet high. Here, about these hills, dwelt, in the early part of this century, the world-famous fortune-teller, Moll Pitcher ; her real name was Mary Diamond. A person of very little education, she possessed a keen perception and reflective qualities. She died April, 1813, aged seventy-five years. Lynn, at the present time, is a flourishing, well-populated city, given to the manufacture of shoes, principally. Passing along the water front of the city of Lynn, with its wharves, we come to the low, marshy shores of West Lynn. Here is located the West Lynn yacht club, much smaller than its neighbor, and very much younger. The shore, low and marshy, now runs in a very irregular way, in a southwest direction, to the mouth of Saugus River. On the opposite side of its mouth is the summer resort called the Point of Pines. It has numerous trees, extensive and well-cultivated gardens, two tasteful hotels, a beautiful beach, and amusements of all kinds to attract the summer visitor or occasional excursionist. Point of Pines is situated at the end of Revere Beach, in the town of Revere, — considered, by many, the finest beach around Boston. The narrow gauge railroad traverses its whole length, and, within a few years, numerous small hotels have been erected on its shores. It is two miles long, and its hard, smooth sand is particularly adapted for carriages and horses. At the southwest end of Revere Beach, the shore makes an abrupt turn, is high land, and terminates in a point. There has been built, within three years, a long pier or wharf, called Ocean Pier, to which a line of excursion steamers has been run from Boston. On this pier has been built a large pavilion, where roller-skating, dancing, and concerts attract many excursionists. From this point the shore runs to another headland, called Grover's Cliff, a hill one hundred feet high, and containing nearly one hundred and eighty acres. The shore between these two points or headlands is called Crescent Beach, and the highlands are laid out into quite an extensive settlement, called Beachmont. The shore now recedes to another point or headland, called Winthrop Great Head, and thence to Deer Island, or Shirley Gut. This peninsula is half a mile long and about a fifth of a mile wide, one hundred feet high, bare of trees. The headland has a precipitous face or bluff. On the eastern side of this head is a hard, sandy beach, which, within the past five years, has become a favorite summer residence of Boston people. Here a good sized village, named Ocean Spray, has been laid out. Its streets are lined with many pretty cottages and two commodious hotels. Point Shirley is separated from Deer Island by Shirley Gut, the narrow strait with swift current hitherto described.

The shore from the Gut runs northwest and north, then makes a sharp turn to the southeast and northeast toward Winthrop Great Head. About the middle of the eighteenth century a short-lived attempt to establish a fishing town here was made, and the experiment inaugurated with great *éclat*, the Governor and many of the prominent citizens of Boston being present; but, from the repute the place acquired from such an opening, it soon became a favorite summer resort, and it was given its present name, Point Shirley, in 1753, in honor of Governor Shirley. In early times the point was covered with trees. In 1776, off its shores, was fought a deadly fight between boats of the British fleet and two Continental privateers. In 1812 a fort was built on the hill to guard the entrance of the Gut, and later, salt and copper works were established. The remains of the buildings and wharf are still standing at the present time. The low lands of the point are now occupied by the Point Shirley House, familiarly known as "Taft's." Its genial proprietor has catered for over twenty-five years at this point, and his game and fish dinners are known all over the world. On the western side of the narrow neck of land connecting Point Shirley with Great Head, is situated the Great Head Yacht Club, an organization only formed in 1884, but possessing the energy to make it a club of importance. We now come to the town, itself, of Winthrop. Although the name Winthrop applies to nine hundred and eighty-nine acres of land, with eight miles of beach, this portion is the head and centre. Of its early history but little is known. Tradition connects it with being the place where some of the treasure of Captain Kidd was buried. During the siege of Boston it was the residence of many refugees from the city. Many old residences remained standing until within a few years. The old Deane Winthrop's house, near Ocean Spray, was built in 1649. Winthrop forms the northern boundary of the inner harbor of Boston. The shore now takes on to Breed's Island, now part of Boston. It seems a part of the main land, but it is separated by an arm of the harbor, narrow as a creek, which makes in on its southeast, east, and northeast side, and on the north-northwest by Chelsea River. This island was called, originally, Susanna Island, from the daughter of Sir William Brereton, early mentioned in the history of East Boston. In 1800 John Breed, an Englishman, bought the island, built a dwelling two hundred feet long and one story high, and resided here for many years as a hermit. From Breed's Island we come to East Boston, otherwise Ward One of the city of Boston, passing by the new East Boston park, opened only this year, and the new settlements of Wood's Isles and Harbor View, built upon the two points of the land. This is an island similar to Breed's Island. The part that joins Breed's Island is very low, flat, and marshy, excepting the bluffs on which the previous named settlements are located. It is bounded on the other

side by Chelsea River, separating it from the city
of Chelsea. The other parts of the island are
higher ground, terminating on the north and south in
high hills. The whole western side, which faces
Boston proper, is lined with fine wharves, covered
with a grain elevator and warehouses for storage, and
traversed by the tracks of the various railroads, by
which freight, direct from the far west, is delivered to
the vessels at the docks. This island was known as
Brereton Island in 1628, from Sir William Brereton, to
whom it was granted by John Gorges. In 1629 it was
called Noddle's Island by the early settlers, after William Noddle, a bachelor, who, it is said, first occupied
it as a habitant. In 1629 the island was occupied by
William Maverick, a refugee from the Dorchester
colony. The name has been cherished, and some of
the public buildings bear his name to this day. In
1633 the General Court granted the whole island to
Maverick for the yearly payment of a "fat wether, a
fat hog, or forty shillings," to be paid the government.
Maverick, like his neighbor, Thomas Walford, of
Charlestown, had strong Episcopal opinions. This
being disliked by the other residents, he was forced to go
to New Amsterdam, where he afterwards lived and died.
During the siege of Boston, in early Revolutionary days,
it served as a refuge for the inhabitants of Boston. At
this time the island possessed a great number of horses
and cattle, which being coveted by the British soldiers,
caused the *second* battle of the Revolution, and the
first where American artillery was brought into play.
In 1780, barracks were built for a hospital for the
sick of the French fleet, and about this time the island
was fortified. They continued to be used until 1833,
when they were allowed to drop into decay. In this
latter year, it is said, the island possessed but eight
inhabitants ; but two years later the records report
over six hundred. East Boston, outside of its freight-

ing facilities, is a manufacturing town. Here, in days before iron was so extensively used, it led the world in the building of clipper ships, whose fast sailing was the wonder of the age. Some remains of this industry are visible at the present day. East Boston was, until recently, the sole landing-place for the European steamers; but the building of the extensive docks on the South Boston flats has given her a rival. The extreme southwestern point of the island is called Jeffries' Point; here is situated the Jeffries Point Yacht Club. The island is reached from Boston by three ferries.

At the upper end of the inner harbor of Boston
Chelsea. beyond East Boston, and lying at the junction of the Mystic and Chelsea Rivers, is the city of Chelsea, connected with East Boston and Charlestown by bridges. The Indian name of Chelsea was Winnisimmet. The whole of the towns of Winthrop, Revere, and Chelsea were under the same town government whose head centre **was at** what is now called Revere. The city has two prominent hills, the one nearest the Mystic now occupied by the Marine Hospital, and Powderhorn Hill on the east side of the city. The building on its summit, originally a hotel, has since 1882 been bought and used for the Soldiers' Home. In 1775 the principal settlement was at Revere, and what is now Chelsea consisted of four farms owned respectively by gentlemen by the name of Williams, Shurtleff, Cary, and Carter. In 1837 a company was formed for the settlement of this part of the town, which bought the ferry which ran to Boston, and Williams' farm. In 1835 the same company added the Shurtleff farm, and the land was laid out into house lots ; from this settlement arose the present city of Chelsea, incorporated March 13, 1857. Across the mouth of the Mystic River we come to the historical whilom city of Charlestown, now the 3d, 4th, and 5th wards of the city of Boston ; it forms

the head of Boston Harbor, and is situ- **Charles-**
ated at the junction of the rivers Charles **town.**
and Mystic. This was anciently the camping-ground
and headquarters of the chief of one of the Massachusetts Indians. Its name was then Mishawam.
The first white settler is supposed to have been
Thomas Walford, who came from the Weymouth
colony in 1625. His Episcopal beliefs caused con-
flicts with the early colonists here, and he was forced
to remove to Portsmouth about 1633, where he died (it
is thought) about 1660. The first permanent settlement was made in 1629, when Thomas Graves, a skil-
ful engineer from Gravesend in Kent, laid out the
town. The colonists, about one hundred in number,
had previously arrived at Salem. The name given to
the settlement was Cherton ; by some it was called
Charlton, and Charlestown. Governor Winthrop in
1630 landed here and intended to make the place the
seat of government, but from the scarcity of good
water he soon after removed to Boston, or Shawmut as
it was then called. The territory comprised within
the limits of the town extended nearly eight miles
from the centre on both sides of the Mystic, an area
that is now covered by at least a dozen cities and
towns. In 1636 Lovell's Island belonged to the town.
It was here, within the limits of this town, that Governor Winthrop built the first ship ever built in Massachusetts, the " Blessing of the Bay," launched July 4,
1631. The town was originally laid out with streets
around a hill in the form of an ellipse and it was mu-
tually agreed that each inhabitant should have two-
acre lots to plant upon. Shortly after, some began to
build in a straight line upon their lots, and this was
the commencement of what is now the principal street
of the city,—Main Street.

Upon the removal of Governor Winthrop, Increase
Nowell, one of the assistant governors, was the only

one of the government officers who remained here. He was secretary of the colony for many years, and has been regarded as the father of the town and church. Rev. John Harvard became a resident of the town in August, 1637 ; at his death he bequeathed one half of his estate and his valuable library towards the foundation of the college that now bears his name. He lived on what is now called Main Street. A monument was erected to his memory in the ancient burial ground, Sept. 26, 1828. In 1630 a fort was built on the Town Hill, the men, women, and children lending a hand in the work. This fort was abandoned about forty years later. In 1634 a battery was built on Sconce Point, near our Warren Bridge. In 1774 the guns were secretly removed, to prevent their falling into British hands. The town, from its earliest settlement, paid great attention to its militia, and a training-field was early established. Every Friday was the field-day, and it is said that the town possessed the best horse troops in the whole colony of Massachusetts Bay. Charlestown has three hills of prominence, all of them named from the early owners of the land,—Bunker Hill, one hundred feet high ; Breed's Hill, sixty feet high ; and Moulton's Hill, forty feet high. The town was the terminus of the first ferry from Boston in 1631 ; this was granted to Harvard College in 1640. The first dry-dock in the whole country was built here. In October, 1801, the United States government purchased some land for a navy yard, which has been added to it later. The present navy yard contains 87½ acres and has a water front of 8,270 feet ; it includes numerous stone, brick, and wooden buildings ; the grounds are handsomely laid out with stately trees. The finest ropewalk in the country is in this yard ; it was built in 1836, of stone, and is 1,360 feet long. Another building has been erected recently for the manufacture of wire rope. All the rope used by the United States government is made in this yard. The story of the first battle of the Revolutionary War is too familiar to relate, suffice it to say that the imposing stone monument (completed in 1843, and cornerstone laid June 17, 1826) rises in majestic grandeur, a fitting land-mark for this old town as well as Boston Harbor.

Boston proper forms the extreme western boundary of the harbor which bears its name. It formerly was a small peninsula of about 625 acres, connected with the main land by a narrow neck only a few yards wide, bounded on the north and west by Charles River, on the east by the harbor, and on the south by a cove or bay. This peninsula was divided into two peninsulas by the mill-pond on its north side, and the town cove on its eastern side. These were connected by an artificial creek called Mill Creek, situated about where Blackstone Street is at the present day. By the filling up of the coves, the present area of the peninsula is nearly three times as large as when it was first settled. It was totally destitute of trees, and its surface was covered with a growth of small bushes. Town Cove, on the harbor side, was the principal landing place. Its northern point was Copp's Hill ; its southern, Fort Hill ; and it made into the land one-eighth of a mile, as far as the present Faneuil Hall. The northern cove or mill-pond had for its extremities Copp's Hill on the east, and on the west a point situated where the present Bowdoin Square now is ; the western shore was washed by Charles River, now Charles Street ; the southern bay started from the foot of our present Summer Street, followed along our present Beach Street and Harrison Avenue to the Roxbury line. Boston's Indian name was Shawmut ; it was afterwards called by the early settlers, Tri-Mount or Træmount, from the three hills which it possessed.

It took its present name by the act of the government, Sept. 17, 1630 ; for most of the settlers came from Boston, England, and furthermore Lady Arabella Johnson, wife of one of the assistant governors of the colony, was a native of that town.

The three hills of Boston were Beacon, Fort, and Copp's hills.   The first was originally called Sentry Hill, and afterwards Beacon Hill, from the beacon that was erected upon its summit ; it was subdivided into three distinct hills,— Beacon, the highest, being two hundred feet high (considerably cut down in 1824); East, Pemberton, or Cotton's Hill, the later name from Rev. John Cotton ; and West, Copley, or Mount Vernon.   Cornhill or Fort Hill was eighty feet high. The first name was given it from the quantities of corn planted there, and the later name from the fort that was early erected upon its summit ; Snow Hill, Windmill, or Copp's Hill was fifty feet high ; it was called Windmill Hill from a windmill that was erected upon it in August, 1632.   The name Copp's Hill was given, it is supposed, from William Copp, a shoemaker and elder of the church ; Copp's Hill was in the centre of the northern peninsula of old Boston.   There were several smaller hills situated at the foot of the Common, only two being left at the present time.   The two hills, Fort Hill and Copp's Hill, resembled two sentinels guarding the cove of Boston, while Beacon Hill stood as the rear or a reserve guard.   The first settler of Boston was William Blackstone (Blaxton as called by some historians), one of the colonists of Sir Ferdinando Gorges' settlement at Weymouth in 1623, and came here in 1625.   He is described as a bachelor, thirty-five years of age, who spent his time cultivating the land and trading with the Indians.   In 1634 he sold to the colonists all but six acres of his land and removed to Rhode Island, and afterwards married a Boston lady and died at Cumberland, R. I., May 26,

1675. In 1684 the remaining six acres came into the possession of Boston.

The next settlement of Boston was made by Governor Winthrop's party some time in September, 1630. These colonists sailed from Southampton, England, March 22, 1630, and arrived at Salem June 12 the same year. It was their first intention to remain together, but some went to Mystic (Medford), Noddle's Island (East Boston), Mishawam (Charlestown), and others to Watertown, Roxbury, Dorchester, and Saugus River. The settlers of Boston were from Charlestown, coming here owing to the abundance of fresh water on the peninsula.

The settlement grew fast, and, as its leader was the appointed governor of all the colonies in Massachusetts Bay, it acquired the position as seat of government which it has still retained. Soon after settlement the colonists prepared for attacks by building forts and other means of defence. May 24, 1632, the fort on Fort Hill was begun, persons from all the settlements taking a share in the work ; and on Oct. 26, 1687, a fort with bastions was built, with a house for the garrison ; this was called " The Sconce " or South Battery. The North Battery on Copp's Hill was erected in 1646. In September, 1673, a stone and wooden wall was commenced, and extended across the Town Cove from the North to South batteries, it was 2200 feet long, twenty-two feet wide, and fifteen feet high, and had a gate or bridge to admit boats into the cove. This barricado, as it was called, was manned with guns and had numerous breastworks. All these defences were given up soon after the Revolutionary War, and the forts farther down the harbor took their place.

Boston in early days had no communication with the main land except at the neck on its western side, and by boats to towns on the opposite shores. In November, 1637, the first ferry was started to run to Charlestown, and in September, 1638, others to Chelsea (Win-nisimmet), and East Boston (Noddle's Island).

The first bridge was Charles River Bridge, finished June 17, 1786; followed by Warren Bridge, 1793 ; Dover Street, 1804; West Boston, 1805 ; Craigie, 1809; Mill Dam, now Beacon Street, 1821 ; Federal Street, 1828 ; Chelsea, 1834 ; Broadway, 1872 ; Congress Street. In 1858, toll bridges were made free. As has heretofore been mentioned, a great deal of present Boston is made-land. The present Causeway Street was built as a dam for the Mill Pond, and the borders of the pond were the site of many mills, whose sluice-ways emptied into Mill Creek, which emptied into the Town Cove. Broad Street was built in 1837 ; India Street, 1838; and Atlantic Avenue is of very recent date. Long Wharf was the first wharf built (1709), started from what is now Merchants' Row and extended 2000 feet into the harbor; on either side of its end was an island or rock.

In 1641 the first ship was built in Boston ; it was of one hundred and sixty tons burden and commanded by Capt. Thomas Graves. This same year, 1641, the first rope-walk was built by John Harrison. John Foster, of Dorchester, established the first printing office, December, 1674; previously the only one in the colonies was at Cambridge under protection of the government, and operated by an Englishman. As there was no wood upon the peninsula in early days, the settlers had to procure it from the adjacent town and islands ; many laws were passed requiring said towns to furnish so many cords of wood.

Boston furnishes us many lessons in the history of the Revolutionary War. Here was shed the first blood. Here were stationed the first British troops and on Liverpool Wharf (then Sargent's,) was held the noted "Tea Party." In the war of 1812 it took a leading part, and in the late civil war its history is well known.

The events clustered around this city would require pages to do it justice, but time and space forbid us to linger longer. Let us now pass across Fort Point Channel.

The southern shore of Boston proper is washed by the waters of the South Bay or Cove ; its outlet is called Fort Point Channel. Across Fort Point Channel we come to the new docks of **South Boston** Boston, built on the recently filled flats of **Boston** the peninsula of South Boston. Ten **Docks.** years ago the great undertaking was begun. Massive

stone piers have been built almost to tide water, where the largest steamers can land their freights and receive return cargoes from the railroads that traverse the wide continent. Immense freight-houses and a large grain elevator have been built on these piers. This immense undertaking is at present but in its inception ; for it is intended to extend the system of piers as far as the shore of City Point, the eastern extremity of the peninsula.

South Boston. The southern portion of the city of Boston is an extensive peninsula, washed on the north by South Bay, and on the south by Dorchester Bay, it is connected with the city proper by four bridges. Its Indian name was Mattapannock or Mattapan, and in later days it was called Dorchester Heights, being a part of the town of that name. In 1660 the first building was erected by Deacon James Blake ; there were only nine houses on its

vast surface in 1776. In 1776 it was brought into much prominence by 2000 Continental troops occupying its heights and throwing up fortifications in one night, thereby compelling the British then occupying Boston to evacuate the city, and finally leave the harbor altogether. The peninsula was annexed to Boston in 1804. It then had only nineteen voters, and to-day its inhabitants number nearly 75,000.

City Point. The outer or easterly part of the peninsula is called City Point, and off from it, across the shoals, is Fort Independence. Upon the

extreme point is laid out a park, whither multitudes
flock during the summer to enjoy the sea breezes and
charming views. On the highland is situated the
Blind Asylum, an imposing white building. On the
southern side of the peninsula is the favorite anchorage and harbor for a very large fleet of yachts of
every kind. At the height of the summer season
some 700 or 800 yachts lie moored here. Here are
located two yacht clubs. The Boston Yacht Club,

organized in 1866, the oldest in New England, is
the sole owner of a fine house and considerable land,
and has a large and enthusiastic roll of members,
comprising many of Boston's merchants. The South
Boston Yacht Club is a younger and smaller club
but quite active.

From City Point the shore runs to the westward for
a mile and a quarter, then turns to the southward for
half a mile, and then to the eastward into a long

marshy point (Cow Pasture or Old Harbor Point),
Old Harbor. thus forming a large, but shallow bay, dry at low water, called Old Harbor. On the northern shore of this bay are situated the yacht-building yards of many well-known builders. The **Cow Pasture.** southern shore is called Cow Pasture, and is the site of the pumping station of the new Boston sewerage system. The buildings were erected within the past few years at a cost of over one million dollars, and the whole system cost over seven millions. A tunnel starts from here and runs under Dorchester Bay to Moon Island, a distance of one and a half miles. This tunnel is 150 feet below the water, and is seven feet in diameter.

A small cove dry at low water makes in between the southern side of this point and a steep, partly wooded acclivity called Savin Hill, one hundred feet in height. **Savin Hill.** Before the establishment of the new sewerage system this hill was considered a most enjoyable place of residence, there being a good beach, offering all the pleasures of the sea-shore. In 1776 a part of the Continental army occupied this hill during the siege of Boston. The shore from here extends to the eastward from the base of the hill into a long narrow sand-point called Savin Point, and on the southern side a cove, dry at low water, makes in, which is crossed by the Old Colony Railroad. Savin Hill is the northern part of Dorchester, and is the only high land on the coast until Squantum (part of the town of Quincy) is reached.

Dorchester. The original area of this portion of the city was immense, it covered a district thirty-five miles long, and is stated to have extended within one hundred and sixty rods of the Rhode Island line. The old town comprised what is now South Boston, Washington Village, Harrison Square, Meeting House Hill, Savin Hill, Mount Bowdoin,

Mattapan, Neponset, and Squantum, and a portion of what is now Hyde Park. The first-named district was annexed to Boston in 1804, the next in 1855, and all the rest, except the last, in 1869. Squantum was annexed to Quincy and Hyde Park in 1855 and 1868. Milton and Stoughton (set off, 1726) were once included within its boundaries. The town belonged to Suffolk County until 1793.

There were in the town, in 1765, 204 houses and 1360 inhabitants. Dorchester joined heartily in the war for independence, and within its limits (Dorchester Heights) was the scene of many camps. On these heights was thrown up the redoubts and planted the cannon which enabled Washington's army to force the British to evacuate Boston.

The first settlement of Dorchester was June 6, 1630. Rev. John White, of Trinity Church, Dorchester, England, was the promoter of the emigration of the colony. A company of about one hundred and forty sailed from England in the ship "Mary and John," under the command of Capt. Squab, March 20, 1630. The reluctance of the captain prevented their entering the harbor, and they landed at Nantasket Point, then a wilderness, May 30, 1630. Procuring a boat from some of the old settlers, they loaded it with goods and started up the harbor (they believing it to be Charles River), landing at Charlestown. A part of the party went up Charles River until it began to be too narrow; here they landed and were met by an Indian holding out a fish, which was exchanged for a biscuit. (This scene is depicted upon the seal of Watertown of to-day.) They soon returned to Charlestown, where they joined their party, and next landed at a place called by the Indians Mattapan, now South Boston. A week from their arrival at Nantasket all their goods were removed to their new settlement. One week after, Gov. Winthrop arrived at Salem.

Dorchester was the first settled place in Suffolk

County, and was given its name by the Court, Sept. 7,
1630. In July, 1633, a new arrival of eighty more
made the town the largest and wealthiest in Massachusetts. In all military and civil meetings Dorchester stood the first, and received the first town government in New England, Oct. 8, 1633. On May 30,
1639, they passed a tax levy for the maintenance of
free schools. This was the earliest movement for the
establishment of free schools that has made New
England so famous.

Fishing was a very lucrative occupation for the
inhabitants of Dorchester. The early houses were
simple log cabins covered with thatch. The oldest
house was the Minot House, which many of the
present inhabitants can remember ; it was burned
November, 1879. It appeared all wood, but its frame
was filled with brick, either for durability or for
protection from assault. Other ancient houses remained until within a few years. Dorchester had the
first church in the Bay. It was built in 1631. It was
used at one time as an arsenal. This stood for fourteen years, when a new house was built on Meeting
House Hill. This hill has remained a site for a
church for 210 years. The first minister was Saul
Maverick, who afterwards settled at East Boston.

Dorchester was expected to become the chief place
and common centre of Massachusetts, but the meagre
depth of its harbor prevented its development as a
political and commercial capital. Annexed to Boston,
June 22, 1869. Dorchester is a favorite place of
residence for the business men of the city. From
its highlands one obtains charming views of the
harbor and the adjacent country, while its numerous
historical mansions and places are interesting to all
students of colonial life and times.

The southern point of the entrance to Quincy (?)
Cove is a flat peninsula called Commercial Point. It

forms the western shore of the mouth of the Neponset
River, and consists of lowlands thickly set- Commercial
tled. There is a wharf on its southeastern   Point.
part. On the shore of this cove or bay is the thickly
settled part of the town known as Harrison Square.
Here is also situated another flourishing yacht club
called the Dorchester Yacht Club.

Inland from the bay are the high lands of Mount
Bowdoin and Meeting House Hill, from the summit of
which are had some remarkably fine views of the harbor.

Neponset River leads to Neponset Village, now
part of Boston, which is one mile above its mouth ;
two miles further is Milton Mills. The   Neponset
river is narrow and crooked, is one third   River.
of a mile in width at its mouth, and about thirty miles
long. In early days many mills were built on its banks.
On the eastern shore of its mouth are extensive salt
meadows known as Farm Meadows, forming a peninsula called Farm Point ; adjoining them to the eastward is another peninsula called Squantum. It is
irregular in shape, extending in an east-northeasterly
direction, and is about a mile in length, with an
average breadth of two thirds of a mile ; it is hilly, and
has a bluff one hundred feet high on its water front.
A short distance to the north is Thompson's Island,
and connected with this peninsula by a flat dry at low
water is Moon Island. According to one tradition it
was named from Tisquanto, an Indian chief, the first
to make friends with the early settlers. In 1776 the
place was the scene of some cannonading by the British vessels. In 1812 the first race-course in the State
was established here. Squantum has always been well
settled, and many fine residences have been built, but
by the establishment of the sewerage system on Moon
Island its reputation for a summer home is forever lost.
Squantum forms the boundary of Dorchester Bay on

the north and Quincy Bay on the east.   Squantum was
annexed to Quincy in 1855.   From Squantum peninsula the shore runs nearly in an easterly direction
for about two and a third miles to Hough's Neck, a peninsula of Quincy which forms the easterly boundary of
Quincy Bay.   This shore is mostly low-lying and highly
cultivated.   A little back of it rise several hills, chief
among them being Mount Wollaston.   It is situated
at the point where Hough's Neck joins the mainland, and
was named after Capt. Wollaston, who settled here in
1625.   This was also the site of the first settlement in
Boston Harbor.   In 1622 Thos. Morton, of London,
obtained the government of this colony and led the
colonists into scenes of such frightful debauchery that
the Pilgrims formed an expedition to break up the
colony ;   they landed here, arrested Morton, and
burnt the place.   Edmund Quincy died in 1636, aged
33 ;   by his death his son, Edmund Quincy, Jr., came
into possession of 1000 acres ;   the property still
remains in the possession of that family.   From
them the town was named Quincy.   The town of
Quincy proper is situated about a mile in the interior ;
it has no approaches by water, but is situated on a
small creek emptying into the Weymouth Fore River.

Wollaston Heights, another section of the
Wollaston Heights. town, is also situated in the interior ; from
its eminence it is quite a prominent land-
mark in the harbor.   Atlantic is another section newly
settled.   Blue Hills are to the westward ; they offer an
important landmark to vessels entering the harbor.
They are 635 feet high, and cover a space of about
twenty square miles.   They are not only noted for
their grand height and beauty, but for the rich stores
of granite which they contain.

Hough's Neck, so-called for Atherton Hough of
Boston, to whom it was granted in 1637, is a peninsula
one mile long, of moderate height ; at its northeastern

end is a hill one hundred feet high, with a steep bank,
this is called Quincy Great Hill. Hough's Neck
forms part of the western boundary of Hingham Bay,
a sheet of water bounded on the south by Weymouth and Hingham, east by the western shores of
Nantasket Beach (Hull), north by Hull from Windmill Point to Point Allerton, west by Pettick's
Island and Hough's Neck, dotted by many islands, having narrow channels bordered by numerous flats, covered with grass, and which are always covered by water.
After leaving Quincy Great Hill, the shore runs south
to another point of land called Rock Island Point or
Head ; this land is sixty feet high. This point is at
the mouth of a river called Weymouth Fore River ;
from here, the shore makes an abrupt turn westerly,
and thence easterly, making a cove called Rock Island
Cove. On the opposite side of the cove from Rock Island Head is a small village called Germantown. This
place was settled by German and French Protestants.
In 1776 it took an active part in the Revolution and sent
out some privateers ; it was quite early a **Gull**
seafaring place, and many ships were built **Point.**
here in later years; it is situated on a peninsula, at
the end of which is a point called Gull Point ; this
peninsula is low land ; the shore from Gull Point runs
southwest to Town River Bay, thence follows the bay in
a westerly direction to a point of land called Phillips
Head, which is the entrance of a cove called Sailors'
Snug Harbor, which is only a harbor in name, for the
cove is dry at low water. Here is the home for poor
and aged sailors, founded in 1856. Town River
Bay is 175 yards wide at its entrance ; then, widening
to an eighth of a mile, it extends one mile in a northwest direction, at the head of which empties Town
River, on which Quincy is situated. On the shore of
the south entrance is the village of Bent's Point ; here
a bridge crosses Weymouth Fore River, which is an

eighth of a mile wide at this point. The river, after
leaving the bridge in a southerly direction, widens into
a bay. A little way south of the bridge is Ruggle's
Creek, a shallow stream running between Bent's
Point Village and a peninsula called Braintree Neck.
On the southern side of Braintree Neck is another
shallow stream called Hayward's Creek, this leads to
Newcomb's Landing; the shore from here runs in an
east-southeasterly direction for a half mile, then south.
Here is situated Weymouth Landing. The river here di-
minishes to a narrow creek. From the landing the shore
takes a northerly course, thence makes a turn south a
little way, forming another cove, into which empties a
North   creek on which is situated North Wey-
Weymouth.   mouth; the shore from here is irregular,
and runs in a northerly direction until it reaches the
bridge opposite Bent's Point. From the bridge the
shore extends in an easterly direction, terminating in a
peninsula called Eastern Neck, which separates the
two Weymouth Rivers, on the northern and western
part of which, opposite Rock Island Point, is a hill
145 feet high, called Weymouth Great Head. Back
from this point, extending to the west, is the village
Old   of Old Spain, the site of the first settle-
Spain.   ment in Boston Harbor, May, 1622; the
extreme point extending from Eastern Neck, and much
narrower than it, is Edward's Neck, sometimes called
Lower Neck, with three points, two extending northwest, and one southeast. This peninsula separates
the two rivers, Weymouth Fore and Weymouth Back.
Here are situated the extensive works of the Bradley
Fertilizer Co. founded in 1861. On the opposite shore
of Weymouth Back River is a wide peninsula separating it from the entrance of Hingham Harbor. Back
River runs nearly south half a mile, then turns abruptly and runs west for five eighths of a mile to a headland
on the southern shore, called Stodder's Neck, a hill

of moderate height, with a cove called Stodder's Cove.
On its easterly side the river then widens out, turns
south, and is crossed, about a quarter of a mile up, by a
bridge, beyond which it is narrow for a quarter of a
mile, then widens somewhat, and is shallow   East and
for three quarters of a mile, beyond which   South
it is nothing but a creek.   On this river   Weymouth.
is situated East Weymouth, noted for its iron works.
The easterly side of the river is high, rocky, well-
wooded, and is a favorite camping-ground.   South
Weymouth is situated in the interior, and is noted for
its shoe factories.

WEYMOUTH.

The first settlement in Boston Harbor was made
in this town, on what is now called Old Spain,
at foot of King Oak Hill, in the middle of May,
1622, by ten men, who came in an open boat from the
coast of Maine, where they had left their ships.   At-
tracted by the beauty of the place, and its position for
trading and fishing, they decided that this site was
worthy to settle on.   The expedition of which they
formed a part was planned by Thomas Weston, an English merchant belonging to the Merchant Adventurers'
Company under whose control were the Plymouth Colony.   Weston not receiving any returns in merchan-
dise from the Plymouth people, sold out his interest
and formed a private company for the establishment of
settlements for trade.   His attempt at settlement here,
and its fate at the hands of the other colonists, have
been described under the heading Mount Wollaston.
After the settlement was abandoned, part of the settlers went to Plymouth, and others to the fishing
stations on the Maine coast.

About the time this first colony was breaking up,
another expedition was being fitted out under the au-
spices of Sir Ferdinand Gorges, who had just received

a patent of a vast tract in this district. The persons who joined this expedition were nearly all of an educated class, among them Rev. Wm. Morrell, Wm. Blackstone, and Samuel Maverick. The two last were the first settlers of Boston and East Boston. All were men of high standing and means, and a portion were mechanics, one of whom, Thos. Walford, a blacksmith, afterwards became the first settler of Charlestown. This party arrived in September, 1623. Finding the remains of the former settlement, and tempted by the shelter which it offered, they established themselves here, and it became the first permanent settlement in Boston Harbor. The Indian name of Weymouth was Wessaguset, and the river was Monatoquot. The town was given the name Weymouth in memory of the town in England.

The shore of the extreme end of the peninsula which separates Hingham Harbor on the east, and Weymouth Back River on the west, runs in an easterly direction to the entrance to Hingham Harbor; here the land makes a point called Crow Point, a hill sixty feet high, with steep banks. A pier or breakwater is built out at its eastern end to the channel. Three eighths of a mile south the shore recedes, making a cove long and narrow, called Walton's Cove. The southern point of this cove is a hill steep on its north side, called Otis Hill. On the southern side of this hill is another long narrow cove called Broad Cove; the shore from this point runs south to the wharves of Hingham.

DOWNER LANDING (CROW'S POINT).

This used to be a favorite landing for the old Boston packets. This land was bought in 1854 by Samuel Downer, who has turned it into a beautiful summer watering-place, containing over ten acres called Melville Garden, which offers attractions of every kind for the excursionist or picnic parties. Ragged Island, a rocky islet three hundred yards long, is connected with the garden by a bridge.

HINGHAM

is beautifully situated, well laid out, with pleasant drives shaded with old trees, and it was once a most fashionable watering-place. The opening and building up of Jerusalem Road in Cohasset, a continuation of the main street of Hingham, has somewhat diminished Hingham's prestige. Hingham was first settled in 1633, and called Bear Cove, from an English town of same name from which the colonists came. Its inhabitants always took an active part in the affairs of the early settlements, and during the Revolution aided the cause in various ways. Many old names which it now contains are descendants of men famous in history. Here is the " Lincoln " family, from which our beloved martyr President descended. It was the birthplace of our war governor, John Andrews, and many others. Many old houses remind us of the old colonial days. The old meeting house, built in 1681, at great cost for those days (£480), is still standing. The old Perry Lincoln house was built in 1640. In the interior is Hingham Centre, South Hingham, still further is Queen Anne's Corner, so called from the houses built in the style of architecture of the eighteenth century. In the extreme southern part is Accord Pond, from which water is taken that supplies the town and Hull to Windmill Point. On the road to Weymouth, on a hill called Fort Hill, are the remains of the old fort built in 1675 for a defence from the Indians. Hingham was the landing-place for the early packets from Boston, the old landing was on Crow's Point, a part of Hingham. In 1818, the sailing boats first made way for the first excursion steamer, *Eagle*.

From the wharves we follow the shore in a northerly
direction to a small cove called Martin's Well, and
thence to a hill called Planter's Hill, one hundred feet
high, which is cultivated on its sides ; this is connected by a narrow strip of lowland to another
hill called World's End, eighty feet high, with a
steep bank on its western side, this hill forms the
limit of Hingham, as Crow's Point does on the south-
Weir ern side of the entrance to Weir River.
River. The shore of this river is the favorite
resort for camping parties. The scenery is grand ; a
branch leads to Nantasket Beach ; the main river
winds in and out among woody hills for some miles
in the interior, and is only navigable for small boats.
The description of Nantasket Beach we will defer
until we trace the shore around the village of Hull.
White On the northern entrance of Weir River
Head. is a narrow neck of high land, extending in
a westerly direction from the beach, called White
Head. Following the westerly shore of the beach,
which runs northerly, we come to Sagamore Head, a
high bluff extending into Hingham Bay, thence to
Strawberry Hill, thence to a low sand point called
Skull Head, and from here to southwestern side of
Point Allerton. The shore from here makes a cove,
which is the northeast point of the bay, thence follows
a pebble beach to the village of

HULL,

situated on four hills, the most northerly being known as
Telegraph Hill. Hull, distant from Boston nine miles
by boat, twenty-two miles by cars, consists of the territory embraced between White Head, Point Allerton,
and Windmill Point on the west, and Black Rock beyond Atlantic Hill, north and east, with Weir River in
its whole length for its southern boundary, seven miles

long and one half of a mile wide at widest part. Hull's first Indian name was Nantasat. Hull was settled, it is said, in 1622, at the time of the first settlement at Weymouth by Thomas and John Grey, and Walter Knight, who purchased it from the Indian chief Chicataubut. In 1629, it was reported by Gov. Winthrop's people as an uncouth place, hardly deserving to be called a settlement. It was formerly thickly covered with wood. In 1644 the Grand Court in Boston ordered one hundred and fifty trees of timber to be cut here to build a fort at Castle Island.

The oldest house is said to be that now occupied by John Boyle O'Reilly, in the village, probably built in 1650; the Nantasket House, quite near this, was built in 1675. The Oregon House was built in 1848 from portions of the old barracks on Fort Independence, it is said. In 1673, Telegraph Hill was covered with cornfields, and a beacon was erected to warn Boston on the approach of danger. In 1776 a French fort was built on the hill by Du Portail, then chief engineer of the army, and it was put under the command of Gen. Benj. Lincoln. From here signals were given to a tower on Central Wharf, Boston. The fort was destroyed at the time of the evacuation of Boston in the Revolutionary war, and was afterwards rebuilt by Count d'Estaing and armed with thirty guns. It is said that the French had a cemetery at the foot of the hill towards the sea, but now nothing marks the place·

The ancient road ran at the base of the hill by this old cemetery. The town has been an Episcopal settlement, a fishing port, a continental fort, and afterward a French camp. Point Allerton is connected with Hull by a pebbly beach calléd Stony Beach. The present point is one half of a mile long. It formerly comprised two hills, and the beacon marks its shoals or point which has been washed away. Its present name was given it by Isaac Allerton of the Plymouth Colony, who explored Boston Harbor in company with Capt. Miles Standish in 1621, who was a relative, and Deputy Governor of Plymouth. In the war of 1776 it was used as a camp for soldiers. The United States government built a strong sea-wall around its sea-front.

NANTASKET BEACH

is four miles long, of smooth hard sand watered on the east by the ocean and on the west by Hingham Bay ; it is devoid of trees, and it affords grand drives, fine sea-bathing. The ownership of this beach was contended for by Hingham and Hull in 1671, but the court supported Hull, insisting that their original grant covered it.

STRAWBERRY HILL

is of considerable prominence, a grassy hill, and not settled at present. The water tower of the Hingham Water Works stands on top. It was the site of a camp of a brigade of Massachusetts militia in 1867. In 1775, an old barn stood on its top and was burned by the Continentals and made a great illumination.

SKULL HEAD,

to the north of this, was the favorite fighting-ground of the Indians, and hence its name. This land has been obtained by a syndicate who have laid out this part of the beach in house lots, and the settlement is called Hobartsville. The next hill to the south is

SAGAMORE HILL,

once the home of an Indian chief, and his great councils were held by him here. The northwest part of this is a bluff called White Head. At the southern end of the beach, in 1826, was a public house opened by a man named Worrick, which was visited by Daniel Webster and all the great men who used to enjoy the shooting on the beach. In 1846 Nehemiah Ripley built the Rockland House, and in 1879 the present Nantasket House was erected The whole beach from Strawberry Hill to Atlantic Hill is now lined with hotels.

ATLANTIC HILL.

The hill at the southern end of the beach is a steep and rocky coast, thickly settled and covered with elegant residences ; it extends south to Weir River, which forms a lake at its base, called Straits Pond or Nantasket Lake. Next beyond this is

GREEN HILL,

forming the other extremity of the town of Hull ; this is thickly settled, but by a less pretentious class. At its southern base is Weir River. This hill terminates and leads on to Jerusalem Road, the aristocratic portion of the southern shore. This road is lined with handsome villas. On a pleasant summer day the travel and fine turn-outs well repays a visit ; the road leads by the Black Rock House, another popular summer hotel, and terminates at the point opposite Minot's Light, on which w_s once the epicures' paradise, Peter Kimball's Pleasant Beach House. The view from this point is one of the finest on the coast, directly out to sea, with the fierce waves breaking with a roar on its rocky coast.